IKIGAI

Find Your Reason for Being

Uncover the Japanese Secret to Happiness and Purpose in Your Life

J. C. LANCASHIRE

Copyright ©2024 J. C. Lancashire
All Rights Reserved

Table of Contents

Introduction 1

Chapter 1: The Fundamentals of Ikigai: Its Philosophy, Historical Background, and Cultural Significance 3

    What is Ikigai? 3

    Historical Background and Its Evolution 4

    How It Became Popular? 5

    Ikigai and Its Significance in the Okinawa Island 6

    Ikigai as a Standard for Attaining Happiness 7

    Ikigai and Other Philosophies 8

Chapter 2: Ikigai and Its Core Elements 13

    The Core Elements/Components of Ikigai 13

    Benefits of Discovering Your Ikigai 18

    Ikigai and The Positive Things It Can Integrate to Your Life 22

Chapter 3: Discovering Your Passion 25

    But What is Passion Exactly? 25

    Is It Different from Hobby? 26

    The Challenge 28

    Self-reflection Tips and Techniques to Identify Your Passion for Ikigai 28

    How to Nurture Your Passion? 34

Chapter 4: Recognizing Your Strengths 37

    How to Identify Your Vocation (Your Personal Strengths and Skills)? 37

    Building on Your Talents 42

    Showcasing Your Strengths 44

Chapter 5: Identifying Your Mission 45
    Understanding Your Values 45
    Finding Purpose Through Service / Mission 48
    Aligning with Global Needs 51

Chapter 6: Balancing Vocation/Profession with Your Skills and Passion 55
    Exploring Career Paths 55
    Achieving Work-life Balance 60

Chapter 7: Ikigai in Different Contexts 65
    Ikigai in Personal Life and Relationships 65
    Ikigai in Health and Well-being 66
    Ikigai and Spirituality 67
    Ikigai in Professional Life 69
    Loving and Embracing the Entire Journey 71

Chapter 8: Living Your Ikigai 73
    How to Incorporate Ikigai Practices into Your Daily Life? 73

Chapter 9: Overcoming Obstacles 83
    Common Obstacles You Will Encounter 83
    Effective Tips and Strategies to Build Resilience and Mental Toughness 87
    Debunking A Couple of Ikigai Misconceptions and Myths 92

Chapter 10: Sustaining your Ikigai 95
    How Can You Sustain Your Ikigai (Sense of Purpose)? 95

Chapter 11: Ikigai in Different Life Stages 105
    Ikigai for the Youth, Teenagers, and Early Adults 105
    How to Practice Ikigai at an Early Age? 106

Middle Age and Finding Renewed Purpose 108
Ikigai During Your Retirement Age 110
Healthy Aging Through Ikigai 111
How to Use Ikigai to Deal with Age-related Concerns
and Challenges? 112
Planning a Great Retirement Through Ikigai 112

Bonus Chapter: Common Japanese Terms 114

Conclusion 118

INTRODUCTION

In this modern age where many question their existence and real purpose in life, it does not come as a surprise if you wake up one day trying to figure out what you really want out of life. You may even be one of the millions of people on a never-ending quest for life's real meaning. It could be that you are still in the dark as to what you truly want, causing you to feel completely empty and unsatisfied.

If such is your case, then you may find Ikigai, which is a famous Japanese concept, a beacon of hope and light. Derived from the Japanese culture, Ikigai has a solid framework for discovering your real purpose and cultivating a more fulfilling and happier life. As a matter of fact, it connects the things that can truly give your life meaning – what you genuinely love, your strengths, what the world specifically needs, and a fulfilling career.

If you master the art of Ikigai, you can connect your societal contributions and personal passions, thereby allowing you to live a richer, more joyful, and purpose-driven life. To make that possible, this book about Ikigai will act as your driving force. This book celebrates Ikigai so much that it will surely touch you and tap into your longing for a more meaningful and fulfilling life.

While reading this book, you will discover that it is so mind-blowing and full of important information that you may end up getting overwhelmed and having difficulty absorbing and taking them all in. If that happens, remember that it's okay as Ikigai is actually a concept that you cannot rush. You should, therefore, slowly absorb the information that this book provides instead of rushing it.

Read the whole book entirely first. Then reread it slower and understand more. Read again until you have grasped its real meaning and see yourself starting to make notes, take action, and develop plans. As you read the book at a slower pace, you will learn about what Ikigai truly is, its fundamental principles, and how you can make it a part of your life. You will get to dive deeper into this concept and even understand its origin and cultural significance. It even teaches you about some challenges you may encounter as you try practicing Ikigai and how you can overcome them.

In the end, you will really gain a deeper understanding of Ikigai and how to use it as your key to finding real joy, purpose, and inspiration. Again, just don't rush the process. Savor and embrace the journey, instead. You reached this point in your life now, which I'm assuming took years. So take your time, thoroughly look within yourself, and ask others for help if needed. Encourage them to search for their Ikigai, too. Only with true soul searching and time will you reap the rewards of Ikigai

CHAPTER 1

The Fundamentals of Ikigai: Its Philosophy, Historical Background, and Cultural Significance

The longing for fulfillment and discovering one's purpose in life is a universal thing. This is true during these modern times when the world seems filled up with all things material that only gives fleeting happiness.

You may have dreamed of building a house of your own, driving your own car, or possessing the things that you were unable to acquire when you were still young, but when you finally achieved that dream, you still feel a kind of emptiness.

You still feel a void and the happiness you get from all those material things seems to fade away in just an instance. This feeling of emptiness may cause you to want something more, forcing you to work even harder to find lasting fulfillment, but to no avail.

What could have gone wrong? The answer could be that you were still unable to find the reason for your being – your life's real purpose. In that case, learning about the Japanese concept of Ikigai can greatly help you. By finding your Ikigai, you get to delve deeper into your sense of purpose, giving you a real reason for living that will not leave you with an empty feeling.

What is Ikigai?

Based on the Oxford English Dictionary, Ikigai is a driving or motivating force represented by someone or something with the ability to give you a reason for living or a mission (sense of purpose). In general, Ikigai also encompasses anything that provides you with total fulfillment and real pleasure.

The word, Ikigai, was also derived from the Japanese words "iki", which means alive or life, and kai, which means result, effect, use, benefit, and fruit. This combination of Japanese words is why Ikigai means the reason for being alive or for living, real life meaning, or anything that makes life worthwhile to live.

Francesc Miralles and Hector Garcia, the authors of a famous Ikigai book, also said that Ikigai, which roughly means experiencing happiness despite being busy all the time, can be likened to logotherapy, though, the former tends to be a notch higher. Many find this concept superior as it provides joy and value to life through people, like your friends or kids, or activities, like your hobbies or work.

Finding your life purpose is usually elusive but doing so is essential as it will let you enjoy a life full of meaning. In most cases, you can find your purpose if you locate what intersects the skills you possess (your strengths) and what you love (your real passion), which is the idea behind Ikigai that offers a more structured approach to making it happen.

Historical Background and Its Evolution

Ikigai originated from the Japanese culture. According to Gordon Matthews, an anthropology professor in Hong Kong who researched Ikigai to learn the tactics used by the Americans and Japanese in discovering their purpose, the first use of the concept can be traced back to the 14th century. You can also see the term being frequently used during the early parts of the 20th century, especially in novels.

Matthews, however, pointed out the lack of details in terms of the historical background of Ikigai and how it was represented in the contemporary works in Japan, like during the 80s, compared to its perception prior to

World War II. Based on his research, he discovered that Ikigai could be linked to the nation and the emperor before the war.

The curiosity behind how Ikigai works, though, only began to get more attention after several decades when there was a noticeable expansion in the standard of living and economy in Japan. Right after World War II, all people were desperately in search of enough to feed themselves and their families, so no one really got the time to wonder what Ikigai was all about.

The widespread use of Ikigai only happened after Japan experienced a significant rise in its economic status and life expectancy decades after the war. As people experienced a higher level of comfort and affluence, they started to question the things that make life worthwhile to live.

Meanwhile, an associate professor and clinical psychologist named Akihiro Hasegawa traces the beginnings of the use of Ikigai to 794 – 1185 CE (the Heian period). According to Akihiro Hasegawa, the meaning of the term "kai" was derived from "shell", a treasure during that time. There were even artists who decorated shells to take part in a game that revolved around matching shells known as "kai-awase". This was one of the favorite games and pastimes of aristocrats during the 11th and 12th centuries in Japan.

How It Became Popular?

Despite the concept starting a long time ago, Ikigai only gained initial popularity in 1966, the time when it went through extensive study and research. During the 1950s, a psychiatrist in Japan, Mieko Kamiya, discovered that even the leprosy patients with mild symptoms who underwent treatment felt like their lives already lacked meaning.

She conducted interviews among these leprosy patients and observed them, leading to her discovery of how Ikigai served as a really vital driving force in finding hope and purpose even when going through terrible experiences, like an illness. The research she made about Ikigai that revolved around that context was actually its first theorized model in Japan.

It then went through a more thorough and extensive development as she wrote "Ikigai-ni-Tsuite" translated as "On the Meaning of Life", a book that really made an impact in the country. Her extensive study even inspired other researchers to continue the work and research. Even present-day psychologists, professors, and researchers in Japan used her study and discovery as references.

Ikigai and Its Significance in the Okinawa Island

Ikigai further evolved, making it a significant structure in the lives of people on Okinawa Island. In the northern part of the island, there was a village known as Ogimi, which was filled with lush forests and took pride in its relaxing subtropical climate. The village became well-known because the people there tend to have a long life plus it had the Shikuwasa, a health-boosting fruit.

The villagers even claimed that their home was Japan's longest-living village. They even had a motto in life set in stone.

> "At 80, you are merely a youth. At 90, if your ancestors invite you into heaven, ask them to wait until you are 100—then, you might consider it."

According to Dan Buettner, a journalist for the National Geographic channel, the long life of Okinawans can be attributed to their strong belief in Ikigai. They made it a point to imbue this concept into all areas of their life.

Ask the villagers about their Ikigai and they will instantly give you a response. They will never run out of answers to the question about what gives their life meaning. It could be as simple as catching fish to feed their loved ones, helping take care of their grandkids, or teaching something to people. The oldest, happiest, and healthiest people in the world are fully aware of the exact reason that drives them to wake up every day.

Ikigai as a Standard for Attaining Happiness

Learning about the way the Japanese follow Ikigai can help you better understand this concept and its complexity. It is the way to find your own Ikigai, too. Based on Japanese culture, a person's well-being has both Ikigai and happiness as its main components.

In that sense, Ikigai has a strong association with certain experiences that come out of future-oriented actions and offer a feeling of genuine happiness and real worth. Many also link Ikigai to the joy and fulfillment that one feels from their perception of such experiences.

Now, how can you link Ikigai to happiness? In areas not part of Japan, people liken Ikigai to the eudaimonic well-being concept while shiawase (happiness) has a closer link to hedonic well-being. If you are still unfamiliar with such terms, you should take note that while hedonic well-being represents a self-serving purpose that focuses on avoiding pain and attaining pleasure, eudaimonic well-being pursues self-realization and a sense of purpose.

Based on the many studies conducted on Ikigai, it was discovered that getting involved in activities that are naturally meaningful daily at home, the community, or the workplace can strengthen one's feeling of happiness and well-being compared to hedonistic actions.

It is crucial to note, though, that Ikigai is unlike those grand things that many feel necessary in discovering their purpose. In fact, it is primarily a spectrum. For over several decades and centuries, many researchers and philosophers tried to respond to what really gives meaning to one's life. Nowadays, there is so much pressure when it comes to achieving success. Our society now tends to have high expectations as far as being successful, whether in relationships, passions, careers, family life, and others, is concerned.

The pressure can be so enormous that it can further result in high levels of stress, depression, and anxiety. You can also see modern places putting more value on matters, like fame, power, and money, causing a sort of disconnection from your true self. With that said, it is no longer surprising to see a lot of people aiming for a more concrete achievement, like a career goal, when trying to comprehend the exact thing that makes it worthwhile for them to live.

Meanwhile, Ikigai has a more unique approach when it comes to uncovering life. In fact, you can find your Ikigai even in the smallest of things. The concept encompasses a rich and wide spectrum, which signifies that your life purpose could be big or small. That said, your Ikigai could be as simple and trivial as your morning cup of coffee, the chance to tend to your garden each day, and the praises you receive for your hard work. No matter how small or big it is, all identified reasons for being have equal importance.

Ikigai and Other Philosophies

Ikigai is not the only first philosophy and concept that aims to help people live a happier, more fulfilling, and purpose-driven life. There are other philosophies and ideas with the same goal – guiding you as you strive for a more fulfilled and productive version of yourself.

Aside from the Japanese philosophy, Ikigai, there is also the Danish tradition called Hygge and the less popular, though equally important, African concept, Ubuntu. All these lifestyle concepts permeate the world as everyone tries to have a better life with the least number of pressure and distractions.

Hygge

The Hygge concept gained global recognition after a few studies discovered that the Southern portions of Scandinavia were home to the happiest people worldwide. Their possessed high level of contentment can be attributed to their solid and firm dedication to the practice of hygge.

Basically, it is taking a moment in your daily life to pause so you can spend quality time with your loved ones. It could be a few moments of enjoying a home-cooked meal. The practice of hygge could also mean spending a moment to care for yourself. You may be able to do this even with just simple things, like reading a book or enjoying tea.

In general, Hygge can be classified as an experience and atmosphere instead of a term referring to things. In most cases, it involves being with your loved ones. The goal is to make you feel like you are in a really loving and supportive home. Hygge also allows you to feel safe. You will feel like you have a shield against the harsh realities of the world and give you the confidence to let your guard down.

Lagom

Lagom also has a different approach to living life happily. Basically, it involves releasing yourself from the negative effects of consumerism and self-indulgence. What Lagom requires you to focus on is searching for balance. In most cases, this concept is described as the "just right" Goldilocks principle. This means that you can't have too little or too much.

When practicing this principle, though, you should remember that the perfect medium differs for each one. You have to go through a personal journey so you can find exactly the perfect medium that suits you.

With its origin in Sweden, which happens to be one of the world's happiest nations, Lagom encourages everyone in the country to practice proper work-life balance. With that, you can see parents in the country enjoying paid parental leave of up to 480 days. You will also have a hard time seeing an employee working overtime. Most of them leave the office at 5 pm sharp.

Unlike hygge, which focuses more on building a more comfortable and cozier environment that promotes contentment, Lagom requires you to look for a more balanced, comfortable, and manageable means of accomplishing things. If you do that, you will have more time to do the things that are more precious to you. All in all, Lagom puts together all the things that many love about the Scandinavian culture, including minimalism, a sense of community, and functional design.

Gezellig

There is also what we call the Gezellig, which came from the Netherlands. Many consider it as vibing. It gives you not only a sense of relaxation and connection but also a feeling of celebration. For instance, a room adorned with lots of gorgeous flowers can inspire those who see it to feel and practice Gezellig. The same can be felt when riding a bike with your best friend or enjoying a potluck dinner with your loved ones.

Ubuntu

Originating from Southern Africa, Ubuntu refers to a strong belief that there is a universal bond and connection of sharing, which is what connects all humans. The roots of this concept can be traced to the humanist African philosophy, specifically the Zulu culture in South Africa, which perceives a sense of community as its society's pillar. The absence of a sense of togetherness also results in the absence of a community.

Oftentimes, Ubuntu is applicable in the work life of business leaders. What they have to do is to consider the elements that make up a sports team. For instance, for a team to win, they need to be consistent in aligning and executing their strategies.

Imagine synchronized swimming as an example. The goal of Ubuntu is to build interconnectedness in each member of the team. It also aims to overcome communication challenges that may cause inefficiency and strife.

Ikigai

As for Ikigai, which is the main focus of this book, most consider it hygge's antithesis. The reason is instead of requiring you to slow down, which is what Hygge is all about, Ikigai encourages you to strive harder to find balance and purpose in your life. You will learn more about this practice and how it intersects four vital elements in human life to find balance in the next chapters of this book.

In general, all the lifestyle philosophies indicated in this chapter, including Ikigai, can be completely customized to fit your unique needs and requirements. Note, though, that no matter how you intend to do it, each philosophy has the same ultimate goal – that is helping its practitioners live a much better and more content life.

Find meaning and purpose in your everyday life as you also cultivate a sense of mission and belongingness both in the workplace and the community. Expect Ikigai, and other similar philosophies, to give you wisdom and guidance during your journey to living the life you deserve.

CHAPTER 2

Ikigai and Its Core Elements

As you may have known by now, Ikigai can literally be translated to life worth, purpose, motivation, or finding happiness through your identified purpose. Note, though, that going through a journey of finding your Ikigai will feel like you are assembling a puzzle. Every piece is significant and once you combine them, you can expect to get the whole picture.

One important point to remember once you find your Ikigai is that it has the tendency to change eventually. This is the reason why you should reevaluate it now and then. Let's say, for example, you have discovered that your Ikigai now is the career you are passionate about. However, once you retire, it is also likely for your Ikigai to change. It is why you really have to understand its core elements/components, so you can always go back to them once you feel like your Ikigai is already changing.

The Core Elements/Components of Ikigai

The Ikigai diagram serves as the heart of finding your Ikigai. Created in the form of a Venn diagram, this serves as a visual tool that aids in exploring the four core elements of Ikigai and how they intersect with each other.

This specific technique of identifying your Ikigai actually came out of the traditional culture in Japan where the concept originated. As you can see in the diagram, it has four questions – all of which you should answer in a certain order. You are also allowed to draw a Venn diagram composed of intersecting circles and then put your answers under the questions in big outer circles. By doing that, you can immediately see the words in the diagram that look opposite or adjacent.

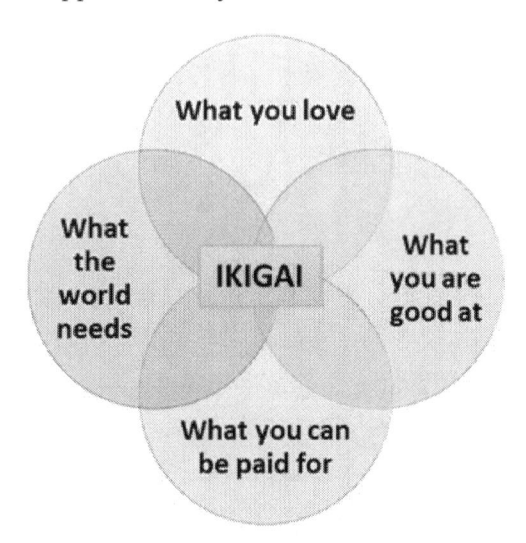

What You Love

The first core element of Ikigai can be seen on top of the diagram – the top circle with the words "what you love". You have to answer this question by identifying whatever it is that you find genuinely motivating, fun, and interesting. This element, therefore, encompasses your passion or anything that truly gives you life.

You will have to identify the exact things that give you genuine happiness. To determine what you love exactly, it helps to ask yourself these questions:

- What do you think you will do in case you no longer have to worry about earning money?
- What will you most likely do during a free weekend or vacation?
- What is the specific thing that excites you and lets out your creative juices?

- What is the topic that you are willing to talk about happily and enthusiastically even for hours?

- What are the activities and tasks that always cause you to lose track of time as you end up immersed in them deeply?

Your passion is any activity or thing that makes you feel alive and excited. It is something you love and have fun doing the most. Your passion for it is so strong that there is a possibility that you will still do it even if you will not receive compensation for it.

What You're Good At

The next core element of Ikigai is your vocation (what you are good at specifically). Once you have explored and identified your passion, your next goal is to assess yourself and determine your skills and strengths. This particular element of the Ikigai refers to the innate skills and talents you have already honed throughout the years. With this element, you will be prompted to explore the knowledge or skills you acquired in a certain area.

For instance, it may refer to your ability to understand complex theories quickly or connect with others. It could also be a specific craft that you have already mastered. With that said, it is safe to say that this element is also the particular zone that makes you feel really competent and confident.

As you try to ponder your vocation, it helps to assess yourself based on the following:

- The specific activities or tasks that you can naturally do with competence and confidence

- An ability or skill wherein you constantly earn praise or compliments

- Tasks or challenges that others find difficult but you can easily and quickly do

Your strengths and skills are those you take pride in as you see yourself naturally excelling in such areas. These could be your learned skills, pursued hobbies, or talents you shared with others when you were still young. It could also be that you have natural skills in writing, music, math, public speaking, painting, or sports.

In addition, this element covers your capability or talent whether it is your passion or not, whether you receive payment for it, and whether or not your community or the entire world needs them.

What the World Needs

Also called mission, this Ikigai element, "what the world needs", is all about exploring the specific needs and requirements of the world. You will also have to figure out the specific area where you think you can confidently create a difference. This element, therefore, already goes over your personal goals and endeavors. What it does, instead, is help you find out how you can offer your service to the world.

Just remind yourself that the world here does not immediately mean the worldwide population. It simply means the community you figured out as you know a problem there that you can solve. To transition to the mission, you should try to contemplate your answers to the following:

- Do you find challenges or problems in a community or the whole world that you really want to solve?

- What are the issues or causes that tend to tug at or touch your heart?

- In what areas do you think and feel you can offer your help through your passions and skills?

- What are the specific moments when you had the urge to make a difference or offer a contribution?

- Does your present work have high demand in the market? Imagine whether your work will remain valuable after one to a hundred years.

- Is your craft or hobby in demand at present?

- Can your craft or hobby solve an environmental, economic, or social issue?

What's great about this Ikigai element is that it can help you connect and communicate with others. In most cases, it is imperative to combine your passion and mission (strengths and skills), so you can use them to do good for those around you. With the help of this Ikigai element, you can reflect on certain changes you wish to make and the things you would like to do to build a lasting and positive impact on others.

What You Can Be Paid For

Also called a profession, the "what you can be paid for" element of Ikigai entails your specific means of living based on your mission and passion. Let's say, for example, you have a talent and passion for singing and believe that your songs can inspire people. Then you can try making a living as a professional singer.

Just remember that it may take some time for you to develop your mission and passion and turn it into a career or profession. No matter how long it takes or how much effort it requires, trust and believe in the process. Also, take note that the possibility of you getting paid for your talent, mission, and passion actually depends on several factors, like how in demand your talents or passions are and the present economic condition.

With that said, this specific element of Ikigai may also include those that can help you make money whether it is something you love and enjoy or not. To uncover this element for you, evaluate yourself through these questions:

- What are the services and skills you can offer to people that are presently in demand?
- What roles do you have or you can do that people will most likely willingly pay you for?
- Do you have passions that you can align with possible sources of income or career paths?
- Do you think you will have a good source of income doing your present job?
- Does your present career give you healthy competition?
- Do you have a craft or hobby that can possibly turn into a career?

If you presently have a job, continue doing it if it can indeed give you a source of income. If you also think your hobby has a chance of giving you a steady flow of income, then you can work on turning it into a dream career. Profession is considered the practical element of Ikigai, which ensures that the things you do will be enough to sustain you whether financially or as far as recognition and resources are concerned.

Benefits of Discovering Your Ikigai

Ikigai is vital in every stage of your life since it plays a major role in your professional and personal growth. You should reevaluate it constantly as it may be necessary to change an Ikigai at one point in your life to accommodate your present lifestyle. Also, take note that you may need some time to locate your Ikigai.

Spend some time writing any phrase, keyword, or idea that you think resonates with you in every circle found on the diagram. After doing that, you should find areas that overlap naturally. Once there are already answers, begin to look at different areas that intersect. Learn about such elements as well as their proven connections. Your goal is to find a balance for each intersecting part. The center of the chart serves as your personal ikigai – the answer and key to achieving a joyful, bountiful, and long life.

However, remind yourself that this Ikigai is unique and only applicable to you. Once you find it, it would be a great move to share it with others. Do so using meaningful communications and interactions as it can help improve life satisfaction.

In addition, if you keep on aligning your life with the core principles governing Ikigai, then you will have to commit to going through a continuous and fruitful process of growth and self-discovery. Once that happens, you will be reaping the rewards and benefits of finding your Ikigai not only for yourself but also for the community.

Promotes a happy life

One major reason why people pursue the Ikigai path is that they wish to enjoy a state of genuine happiness. As you may have guessed by now, the concept serves as one's reason for being. Your Ikigai can also be perceived as anything, which offers you a genuine sense of satisfaction and purpose.

Visualize yourself living while knowing your purpose. This will surely make you feel excited to wake up almost every day. By identifying the specific things that spark joy and happiness in your case, your life will become more meaningful. Such can lead to happier moments. So essentially, your Ikigai serves as your motivator to wake up daily and keep on moving forward.

Helps you find balance

There are several instances when you feel things are already out of your control. Undeniably, you will still experience struggles in life whether or not you have already discovered your Ikigai. As a human being, you are not exempted from going through struggles and pressures now and then. These struggles are also necessary to keep you balanced and grounded and train you to deal with crisis more effectively.

With that said, a lot of people find their identified Ikigai as their catalyst or pick-me-up. If you have a clear sense of purpose, you will also gain proper guidance and clarity. There will always be something that can help you feel rooted. If you find something confusing, your Ikigai will help you find your balance.

Improves your overall health and wellness

Ikigai has several purposes – one of which is to provide you with genuine joy, purpose, meaning, and happiness. Note, though, that it is not the only thing that Ikigai can do for you. It can also give you better health. In fact, many Ikigai proponents apply the concept to their lives to improve their overall health, especially mental, spiritual, physical, and emotional health.

It can keep your chance of dealing with disability low once you reach old age plus it can boost your immunity and speed up your ability to recover from injuries. These positive effects on your health can be attributed to the ability of Ikigai to help its practitioners follow habits and behaviors that improve health. Aside from boosting your physical health, making Ikigai a part of your life can bolster your emotional and mental health.

Keeps your stress level low

It is highly likely for you to experience stress because of your dissatisfaction and disconnection with life. By knowing more about your Ikigai and ensuring that it is in line with the things you are passionate about, your strengths, and the things you love, you reduce your stress. It also promotes a sense of calmness and balance.

The fact that Ikigai brings a sense of real fulfillment can also help make you less stressed in life. It can enrich not only your life but also your loved ones and those surrounding you.

Gives inspiration and motivation

Once you clearly get a grasp of your Ikigai, you can use it as your driving and motivating force to propel you to move forward. Your Ikigai is an incredible source of inspiration and motivation, which can help you move forward no matter how tough things get.

With that, you can also start your journey towards improving yourself. You will experience personal growth as you are motivated to hone your skills, broaden your horizons, and explore new areas in line with your interests.

Promotes longevity

Finding your Ikigai also promotes longevity. It can be linked to a lower risk of mortality caused by life-threatening diseases, like cerebrovascular disease, coronary heart disease, and cardiovascular disease. There is also a low chance for you to deal with functional disability.

There are actually three possible mechanisms that Ikigai uses to help its practitioners have healthier and longer lives. One is that it diminishes the activities performed by your sympathetic nervous system. It can, instead, improve your parasympathetic activities. This makes Ikigai effective in changing your perception of stressors. You can start viewing them as less stressful, thereby aiding you in recovering more quickly. As far as your emotions are concerned, from extremely stressful and adverse situations.

The second mechanism is the ability of Ikigai to reduce the levels of cortisol in your body. This is a good thing as high cortisol is an inflammatory factor that can be linked to cardiovascular disease, low immunity, and hypertension.

Lastly, Ikigai helps you establish a positive psychological state. Here, you will feel like you are really needed, which can enhance your optimism. You also have a sense of purpose, which includes serving the community. With that, you will feel more motivated to engage in productive tasks and activities. This can further lead to a lower risk of experiencing physical disability and dementia.

Improves resilience

Of course, you are aware of the fact that life will always come with a lot of struggles and difficulties. This is the reason why humans keep on searching for things that make life worthwhile and enjoyable. Yes, Ikigai gives the Japanese the kind of happiness and sense of purpose they want but they can't always expect things to be in their favor.

As a matter of fact, you can say that you have the most intense experience when you practice Ikigai if you encounter a sort of life crisis. With that said, expect your knowledge of Ikigai to help you handle even the most complex challenges. You can use it to find meaning in your suffering plus it can build your resilience, thereby empowering you to overcome whatever challenge you encounter in life.

To make Ikigai work for you, you should remind yourself that it can't guarantee that you will have a life with zero pain. What it can do, instead, is inspire and motivate you to take part in more meaningful activities. It will also encourage you to move forward even during your hardest moments. Ikigai can, therefore, provide you with a sense of purpose, as well as the grit to move forward and persevere.

Ikigai and The Positive Things It Can Integrate to Your Life

To the Japanese, Ikigai plays a really major role in their overall well-being. Just like what has been mentioned just a while back, it can bolster your health, lower the risk of disease and disability upon reaching old age, and increase lifespan, thanks to the supreme sense of purpose it provides that will encourage you to take part in activities that promote better health.

In addition, it gives you hope and motivation to persevere and look at a brighter future even at difficult moments. It also boosts your self-esteem and life satisfaction, providing genuine happiness and a sense of well-being and worth to the Japanese.

It is important to note, though, that the difference Ikigai makes varies from one person to another. There is also a possibility that its positive effects on your life will eventually fluctuate. With that said, you really have to keep on rediscovering yourself. You have to find out if the Ikigai you discovered before is still the one that serves as your driving force today. Use the diagram indicating the four vital elements of Ikigai, so you can continue updating yourself about your sense of purpose.

CHAPTER 3

Discovering Your Passion

The first step that you have to take when planning to make Ikigai a part of your life is, of course, to discover your passion. However, if it is still your first attempt to discover your passion, you may find yourself struggling, especially if you are someone who gets easily pressured by your everyday responsibilities and the expectations of society. Sometimes, it can be difficult to discover your passion but with the right tools and techniques, you can identify it and take the necessary step towards practicing Ikigai.

But What is Passion Exactly?

To figure out what your real passion is, you need to have a clear and full grasp of it. Basically, passion can be defined as your deep love or enthusiasm for a certain subject, pursuit, or activity. It is different from interest since passion is a distinguishable part of your personality and identity. It gives your life a solid direction and purpose.

To determine if something is really your passion, you have to look for the following characteristics:

- It greatly excites and interests you.

- It gives you purpose, genuine fulfillment, and joy.

- It takes a significant amount of your time.

- You are willing to pursue even with the possibility of experiencing boredom and setbacks.

Passion is an idea or activity, which consistently and naturally gives you the drive to do things. Once you have identified it, you can see yourself being on your way toward enjoying personal satisfaction and a sense of balance and flow.

Is It Different from Hobby?

The answer is yes. You can distinguish a hobby from your passion based on the depth of your personal and emotional engagement. A hobby is basically an activity you love and enjoy doing for pleasure and relaxation. You often do it during your free or leisure time. It gives you a sort of break from your everyday routine and provides you with satisfaction and enjoyment.

Meanwhile, passion is more intense in the sense that it resonates deeply with your core values and desires. A passion may actually begin as a hobby but eventually, you will notice that it turns into something more important than just a mere pursuit for pleasure.

To make it even clearer for you, here are the primary areas where you can distinguish passion from a hobby.

Commitment and intensity

Each passion comes with an irresistible and strong motivating and driving force that encourages you to rise early each day. Sometimes, it also prompts you to stay up late so you can keep on doing it. Your real passion also has the potential to change your life for the better.

Meanwhile, hobbies refer to activities you also love and enjoy. You find pleasure in them but they are more for recreational purposes. Unlike passion, you don't feel the same strong and powerful urge to do your hobbies.

Sense of purpose

In most cases, a passion also has a deep sense of purpose. It is in line with the principles and values you follow in life and it gives your life more meaning. Yes, hobbies are fulfilling and enjoyable, too, but the sense of purpose they evoke is not as deep. They are not also aligned with your values all the time.

Longevity

Hobbies tend to come and go from time to time. It may also change eventually. This makes it different from passion, which may stick with you for a long time. It is an enduring interest that you can expect it to grow with you and eventually, evolve as you also age.

Emotional connection

Passion is different from a hobby as it tends to have a more profound connection with your emotions. Your passion can even stir your feelings and emotions to the point that you will notice how much they enrich your life.

You will also gain so much satisfaction and the feeling of accomplishment from it. On the other hand, hobbies can give you relaxation and happiness but you can't expect their emotional bond to be as enduring and deep as passions.

How it affects your identity

Another area where you can distinguish your passion and hobby is how it affects your personality and identity. Your passion is capable of exceeding your dream job or career. It will turn out to be an extension and part of your unique identity and personality. It reflects your desires and values and plays a major role in your personal and career growth. Meanwhile, your hobby may not significantly affect your personal evolution or identity.

The Challenge

One thing to remember when it comes to finding your passion is that it may cause you to encounter a few challenges. The most significant challenge you may experience is that you may feel pressured as you try to figure out what it is exactly for you.

Another challenge may stem from the pressure and expectations brought on by society. As you can see, the present society puts more emphasis on traditional approaches and practicality over pursuing one's passion. For instance, you will notice that many find getting a degree at a prominent university more acceptable than getting hired at a coffee shop as you try to go for your dream of becoming a musician.

Another possible problem is one's tendency to put pressure on themselves. You may feel frustrated and begin doubting yourself if you perceive your passion as just one pursuit. This applies to anyone who has a hard time identifying their passion and those who have several hobbies and interests.

You may experience pressure as you attempt to follow one passion in life and view it as a solution for each problem that triggers your anxiety and stress, specifically in a place that has plenty of opportunities and options. This may result in you feeling stuck. You may even feel like you are disconnected from yourself.

Self-reflection Tips and Techniques to Identify Your Passion for Ikigai

Your decision to uncover your passion for Ikigai does not only require you to seek a career path that ignites your passion. It actually entails a journey that requires you to discover yourself. You need to introspect, explore, and muster the courage to go beyond your comfort zone.

So basically, the whole process of identifying your passion requires you to peel back each layer of your pursuits, interests, and desires. That way, you can reveal the thing that you really love. You can't always expect the path to be straightforward but it is very rewarding.

To help you find your passion for the practice of Ikigai, here are some self-reflection tips and techniques you can use:

Practice meditation

One of the most effective self-reflection techniques that you can use to find your passion is meditation. What you should do is make your own mindful life map. In case you are someone who values your creativity, then you can create a scrapbook, which has a visual map of every significant moment of your life – whether it is the high or the low. Include pictures, doodles, snippets, and tickets in the scrapbook.

After completing it, you can take a look back at your life journey so you can search for moments or patterns that give you fulfillment and satisfaction. A few minutes of meditation can even offer you guidance when it comes to having a more mindful reflection. Such quiet and mindful reflections may give you hints regarding your purpose and real passion.

Create your own vision statement

It is also a good idea to write your vision statement – one that really resonates with the life you are living. You can actually do it similarly to how you do it for a company. As you make your personal vision statement, avoid holding back. Let yourself bring out your creativity and dreams. Note that you can start to find your purpose if you let yourself imagine that you are capable of doing anything, which means that this process can also let you enjoy the art of daydreaming.

Begin a passion jar

You can do a self-reflection on what you are truly passionate about by asking yourself about the specific things that make you forget about time. This means that without you realizing it, you are already consuming a lot of time for it simply because you enjoy and love what you are doing. Ask yourself about the things that lighten you up, too.

Write down all your answers on small pieces of paper. Use colorful slips as much as possible then put all of them inside a jar. Draw one slip of paper from the jar every day then do such a task or activity.

Observe your reactions as you draw the pieces of paper. If there are slips that you want to avoid or dread doing, then you may discover how much you need to force yourself to finish it. Eventually, this technique will help you discover the specific activities that excite you and those that don't.

Hone your self-awareness through mindfulness

A great way to build a connection with yourself and learn about what you truly want is to let yourself focus on the now (present moment). This activity is easier said than done, though, so you should prepare for it.

One effective way to make you more self-aware is to do mindfulness. By engaging in activities that make you more mindful, you can connect with yourself even better. You become more attuned with what you want so finding your life's purpose will be easier.

Make a purpose journal

Journaling is also a big help in uncovering your passion. To make it possible, grab a blank journal then ask yourself silly yet profound questions. Put your answers on each page of the journal. Some questions you can ask yourself would be *"If I am a shape, what would it be? Why?"*, *"If I am a song, what would it be?"*, or *"If I become a teacher, what subject will I teach?"*.

You may find these questions trivial at first but once you give honest answers, you will most likely be surprised. The reason is that your answers can give hints or even clear ideas about your passion. Through this journaling exercise, you can converse with your inner self and explore your own dreams, emotions, and thoughts. You will definitely learn about your passion through this.

Determine what you value the most

It's time to reflect and identify the things that are most important to you. You have to be clear about what matters to you the most. Note that passions can always be detected at the crossroads of your real purpose and interest, so determining the things that are truly valuable for you is one secret to uncovering your passion. The following actionable steps can make it happen:

- Explore your own core values – List down your priorities, including your loved ones, family, service, health, innovation, and creativity.

- Define your purpose – Spend time reflecting on your purpose. Go over your overarching calling or mission, specifically the one that provides your life direction and meaning.

- Look back at the challenges you have encountered in the past – Reflect on those you have successfully overcome. You need to list down the major difficulties and obstacles you encountered that you were able to handle.

- Factor in any trigger issues – Which ones among the problems and struggles you encountered stirred an intense emotional reaction from you? Such triggers indicate what matters to you the most.

By doing these actionable steps, you get to unveil certain activities and areas in your life that moved you deeply and intensely, instead of being merely relaxing and fun. This can provide indicators of your real passion.

Determine your competitive edge

It is natural for humans to experience a high level of satisfaction in the things that they excel in. This makes it necessary to understand your own talents, skills, and strengths as doing so can also help reveal your passion. The first thing to do is to assess the strengths that you think are unique and personal to you. Reflect on specific areas where you excel. You can also determine your strong suits by asking for the feedback and opinions of the people you trust.

It also helps to consider the things that you are already knowledgeable about. Think of any useful skill or the ones you learned that have the potential of giving you a lucrative source of income. If possible, take a personality test. The good news is that these tests can now be easily taken for free. You can find personality tests online and take them with ease.

The goal of this test is to help you figure out your personal qualities and traits that give you a unique edge. You will also be able to gain insights into how you can take full advantage of these traits. The good thing about discovering your competitive edge is that it can also help you reveal your passion in certain areas that let you show off your talents and skills. With that, you have a higher chance of achieving success and feeling genuinely fulfilled.

Practice the habit of gratitude

You can also do this activity through journaling. What you should do is keep a gratitude journal and use it to record everything you are grateful for each day. While jotting these things down, do a self-reflection. Try to decipher how every item in the journal aligns with those that really have meaning and value to you.

If you do this journaling activity every day, you will eventually discover patterns. They could be unique passions or recurring themes. Of course, these patterns serve as significant clues in identifying your driving force, the things that make you feel really alive, or your larger purpose. With that, you will find yourself identifying your passion, which is vital for Ikigai.

It also helps to combine the gratitude journaling activity with the habit of maintaining a journal for your Ikigai. In your journal, write the things you love, your strengths, the needs of the world/community, and anything that is emotionally or financially rewarding for you. Here, you also get to uncover a pattern, which will be your guide in identifying your Ikigai.

Do an experiment and explore

Take time to explore various topics, fields, and activities that keep on capturing your interest. Avoid hesitating when it comes to stepping out of your comfort zone. Note that on several occasions, it is worthwhile to push through your nervousness and anxiety.

In case you have spare time, take part in workshops, join community groups or clubs, and read books. If you find the time scarce, listen to related podcasts while driving to or from work and spend time watching instructional videos during your break.

This specific activity is all about self-discovery. You allow yourself to have new experiences that will further hone your growth. Avoid being selective as although these are micro-experiences, they can still help you achieve growth and enlighten you about your passion.

Observe the things that inspire you

It would be a great idea to pay close attention to everything and anything in your life now that sparks something positive within you. The best way for you to start doing this activity is to reflect on what happened in your life so far and look for glimmers of passion that are already present within you. Acknowledge your own hard work as you create that.

It would be best to spend a couple of days (whole days) creating a list of all the small and big things you consider your inspiration. Once the two days are up, begin to observe common patterns and themes. They will act as indicators of your real passion.

Practice getting out of your comfort zone

Make sure that you are willing to push your limits and go beyond what is natural and comfortable for you. According to the famous scientist, Albert Einstein, insanity breeds from doing something repeatedly and then expecting another result.

If you are one of those who operate in a similar way daily and you realize that you can't find your passion through it, then you should be willing to make a change. If that's the case, you should explore areas not part of your comfort zone. Make these activities a part of your routines and you may find it really useful in locating your new inspiration.

Look for kindred spirits

You may want to seek outside help, especially if you have inner work you want to improve and you want to have significant personal growth. In this case, you can work with a therapist, coach, counselor, or anyone who can contribute to strengthening and deepening your self-awareness and deciphering your passion.

Aside from seeking the help of a professional, it is also a good idea to search for inspiration and guidance from kindred spirits whom you admire, respect, and value. It would be a great idea to reach out to people who have the same interests or personalities.

How to Nurture Your Passion?

During your journey towards discovering yourself more, learning about your real passion will surely turn out to be a significant milestone. Your journey, however, does not end with finding your passion for Ikigai. You also need to nurture your passion by building a nurturing environment that will help your passion flourish.

Nurture your passion by making it a part of your everyday life. By doing that, you can live a great life filled with purpose, which can give you a deep sense of satisfaction and fulfillment. You can do this nurturing activity through these tips:

Commit to engaging with your passion regularly

Commit to spending some time with your passion regularly. You should be consistent in this schedule as doing so will be the key to nurturing the growth of your passion. In addition, it can help cultivate a strong and deep bond and connection between your passion (what you love doing) and yourself.

Connect with people who think like you

Be part of groups and communities composed of people with the same passion as you. Participate in events and discussions and take time to share your experiences with them. By establishing a connection with them, you can see yourself enriching your journey towards living life the Ikigai way.

You also get to hear and share various perspectives. This can give you a sense of belongingness, which can significantly improve your mental health and give you the support needed in case your motivation suddenly wanes.

Be open to expanding your knowledge

Once you already identified your passion, commit to growing your knowledge about it. Learn more about your passion. You can attend a workshop, read informative books about it, and take a course. By learning about it continuously, your passion will surely grow and evolve, helping you make the most of it.

Nurture your passion by being kind to yourself

Be patient and remember that the process of nurturing your real passion takes some time. It is actually a long journey. Avoid perceiving it as a race as it has no finish line. It simply does not end. Once you discover your passion for Ikigai, it will be ongoing so exercise patience as you try to cultivate it throughout your journey and make it evolve.

CHAPTER 4

Recognizing Your Strengths

The next thing that you have to do if you want Ikigai to give you favorable results as far as living your life to the fullest is concerned is to recognize your strengths. Again, Ikigai has an important element in the form of vocation (what you are good at). In this case, you should identify your vocation – your strengths and skills.

These are the things and areas where you excel naturally while others are having a hard time. It could be that you have the talent and skill in writing, playing a musical instrument, singing, or playing a specific sport. By learning about your vocation, which is a vital component of Ikigai, you get to tap into your special talents and skills, specifically those that deserve compliments and recognition.

How to Identify Your Vocation (Your Personal Strengths and Skills)?

Everyone has their own skills, strengths, and talents – the ones that we have honed throughout our lifetime that make us unique from the rest. Despite that, many are still unsure of what they can offer to the world. This is why the Ikigai diagram includes vocation as part of its major components.

This particular element of Ikigai requires you to identify and recognize your personal strengths and skills, so you can accept and embrace them more fully. You can then think of how you can apply such skills to things that truly matter to you – your passions.

One way to determine your strengths, if you are still unclear of what those are, is to ask the people around you. Make sure that you ask those you trust for input. They could be your trusted friends, family members, mentors, colleagues, or teachers. Ask them to answer questions with answers that lead you to identify your skills, like the following:

- What areas do you think I excel in? Where am I good at?

- In your opinion, what are the things I enjoy the most?

- What mark do you believe I can leave to the world?

Even if you are already an adult, do not hesitate to ask for such feedback as you are never too young or too old to do this. You can ask for it informally or formally as you converse with people you trust. The ones who already know you so much may clearly see things about you that you can't recognize on your own, thereby pointing you in certain directions or areas you don't expect.

Note, though, that it is not necessary to depend too much on the feedback, especially if you feel like it does not resonate with you. Gathering input and feedback from others is valuable if it gives you a clear idea of your own strengths but if it makes it even more vague, then it is time to look for other methods of identifying your vocation.

Visualize the best version of yourself

Take some time visualizing and imagining the best version of your future self. Make sure that you are very specific when doing this. Think of the best life possible for you in the future. Do a personal assessment and ask yourself about who you would most likely be in the future.

What do you think will be your strengths as you envision your best self? How do you intend to use such skills and talents? Try to imagine where you will most likely be in the future and what exactly you are doing for a living. This self-assessment strategy can give you indicators of your personal strengths and skills.

Reflect on your experiences in the past

By going back to your previous experiences, you can figure out the specific areas in your life where you excel. You can also identify those areas that need improvement. Think of your school and work experiences, as well as the hobbies and activities you did in the past, and assess the areas where you encountered difficulties and saw success.

List down your accomplishments and setbacks. After that, you can start asking yourself about the specific strengths that let you achieve success in such situations. Determine the weaknesses that made it difficult for you to overcome challenges, too.

Take a personality quiz or assessment

It is now easy to access personality quizzes and assessments online that would be of help in uncovering your strengths. Most of these tests, like the Myers-Briggs test and the Wonderlic Cognitive Ability Test, can give you a clear idea of your unique traits, qualities, and strengths. These can also give you a closer look at your weaknesses and specific areas for improvement.

Ensure that when you are answering these quizzes, you are in your best mental space. That way, you can answer the questions truthfully while allowing yourself to do a bit of self-reflection. If you do that, you can always trust the results of the test.

Be more self-aware

It is time for you to cultivate self-awareness as it is one secret to revealing not only your unique strengths but also your weaknesses. Commit to spending a few minutes daily to reflect on your real feelings, behaviors, and thoughts. Make it a habit to ask yourself questions that really penetrate what is inside of you. For instance, ask yourself what prompted you to make a specific decision or what would be your most likely response in a certain situation.

Consider your passion

In the previous chapter, you have learned how to identify your passion. The passion you have discovered will also be of help in revealing your real strengths and vocation, so you have to consider it when doing a self-reflection. Note that if you are passionate about something, you can easily hone the skills and talents necessary in such an area. You can even cultivate them and make them your primary strengths.

Think of the things that you find really enjoyable and do those activities. Pay more attention to the skills that you have to use as you do each activity. Keep in mind that while others naturally have a talent in some areas, everyone is capable of growing their skills and strengths in such areas with time. By uncovering your passion and comprehending your natural skills and talents, you can figure out the specific area wherein you are eager to exert more effort to turn into an expert.

Let's say, for example, you love drawing. You can hone your patience, creativity, focus, and attention to detail by regularly doing it. The good news is that once you hone these strengths, you will be able to apply them in several workplace situations – among which would be graphic design, education, and administrative work.

Your ability to appreciate tasks that others may not like is also a strength. With that said, you should pursue your unique interests, skills, and talents, so you can identify the positive skills you can apply at work, which is also vital in the practice of Ikigai.

Identify patterns

If you have already gathered answers from various sources and areas, it helps to emphasize those that frequently come up or qualities identified by many people. It also helps to reflect on your own by asking similar questions to yourself.

You should then compare their answers and yours to find out if they match. The areas that frequently come up the most are your strongest skills. Your knowledge of your skills can then be used in matching them up with prospective careers.

Evaluate your goals

Take into consideration your set goals so you can reflect on the things to do to attain them. Examine the specific actions and steps you already took for their achievement. You should then analyze the level of success you have already reached so far as this will also help you in figuring out your strengths as well as the areas that still need work.

Determine and accept your personal weaknesses

You may think that this is counterintuitive but identifying your weaknesses can actually help in figuring out your strengths. Once you understand your weaknesses, it will also be easy to look for ways and tactics to overcome them. Reflect on the specific traits that helped you beat such weaknesses.

You should acknowledge and accept your personal weaknesses as it will take you closer to achieving growth. It can give you a more balanced perspective of your own strengths, inspiring you to use and leverage them in those areas and fields where you feel like you are not that good.

Building on Your Talents

Once you have already identified your strengths and talents, it is crucial to integrate them into your everyday life. Making these skills a part of your daily life is an incredible way of honing them. Through constant practice, you can improve your skills and strengths even further, whether it's your communication or problem-solving skills.

Also take note that just like resilience, empathy, decisiveness, and kindness, personal strengths naturally form part of you. They are your innate qualities, too. By learning about them, you can use them wisely, especially in terms of your professional and personal development. With that, you have a much better chance of becoming successful and genuinely fulfilled, which is what you are after when you are practicing Ikigai.

You just have to make sure that you keep on honing your personal strengths as doing such is the key to opening more opportunities for your career plus you get to build stronger and deeper relationships with everyone around you. You can build up your talents and improve your skills even further with these tips:

Focus on being more productive

Avoid overwhelming yourself, though. Now that you are already aware of your strengths and skills, I'm pretty sure that you plan on using them in new ways. However, it is not a good idea to overwhelm yourself and focus too much on improving your skills. Your goal should be to find the right balance as you try to figure out how to make yourself more productive through your identified skills.

Make it a habit to include your strengths in your daily routines. Look for new ways to use your strength in a way that can benefit you every day. Again, avoid overwhelming yourself by overthinking and overanalyzing your actions and behaviors. Doing so may only ruin your self-image and disrupt your hard work, which is not ideal if you are aiming to master Ikigai and make it a part of your life.

Improve through experience

Another thing that you can do to improve your skills and strengths once you have successfully identified them is to gain more experience. For instance, if you were unable to achieve a specific goal, then reflect on what happened and think of ways to use your core strengths to handle a potentially hard and stressful situation.

It also helps to reflect on different ways other people in a similar situation adapt to the challenge. As much as possible, implement the tactics used by your colleagues who have the same strengths and skills as you. It may require asking them questions but, in several cases, you just have to observe the behavior of those around you. This should be enough for you to find out how you can apply such strengths every day.

Embrace positivity all the time

Make sure that you also remain motivated. You need a source of inspiration and motivation as it can help a lot in your journey towards developing your strength. Find out your specific reason for gaining strength and be honest about it.

Is it because you want to achieve progress as far as your career is concerned? Or is it because you want to make yourself more mentally tough as you go through your journey? You are the only one who can find the right answer, provided it resonates within you and gives you the motivation and inspiration you need.

Ensure that your positive demeanor remains, too. Note that there are a few instances when you will experience difficulties identifying your strengths. You may also find the implementation of your soft skills complicated. In that case, you should not worry so much as it is definitely an essential part of your journey.

Eventually, you will gain contentment and satisfaction, especially if you keep going during those difficult times instead of quitting. This understanding can also help a lot in bolstering your persistence, allowing you to push forward as you try to spot your Ikigai.

Showcasing Your Strengths

Since vocation is one of the four pillars of Ikigai, you also have to learn how to showcase it and bring it out to the world. You have to show the world what you are genuinely good at. The people should be able to see a more confident version of yourself who knows exactly your vocation or your strengths and talents.

Showcase your strengths by creating your personal portfolio. It should be able to show what you are truly good at and any relevant training and certifications you receive. This should indicate how much you are committed to developing yourself. Your portfolio also demonstrates how competent you are in the area/s where you think you excel.

In addition, it represents your dedication to stay up to date and current in your chosen field. Don't forget to grab networking and mentorship opportunities as aside from broadening your knowledge and horizon, it can also help you expand your network, making it possible for you to learn from other experts or share your knowledge with others. This can give a superior feeling of satisfaction.

CHAPTER 5

Identifying Your Mission

No matter where you are living, you will always have a role to play in society. Each one of us is a member of society, which means that everyone must also extend help to anyone in need and exert an effort to improve the current state of the world or the community we are in.

You don't have to do something grand to make this happen. You can actually serve the community in your own little way. The only thing that you have to do is to figure out first what the world needs, which is an essential part of Ikigai, so you can also identify your mission. With that, you understand how you can help society using your skills, talents, passion, and available resources.

Understanding Your Values

When it comes to identifying your mission or what exactly the world needs where you think you can offer your help and service, it is important to observe the people surrounding you first. Find out what their needs are and how you can help address such needs.

Make sure to also do things guaranteed to benefit society, such as supporting charities close to your heart, protecting nature, donating blood, and investing in your skills and education. No matter what you choose to do to address the needs of those around you, you have to ensure that it is in line with your personal goals. That said, you need to understand your core values, so you can align them and your personal goals with the needs of your community and the world.

To determine your core values, here are a few tips and exercises:

Make a list of values that resonate with you

Your core values refer to a set of opinions and beliefs that have a huge impact on your way of living. These values have a say in the way you live your life. Such values are so significant as these make up your overall personality and character. Your values also play a vital role in facilitating your response to certain situations and the way you set your goals.

To give you an idea, a few of the many examples of core values include achievement, creativity, care for others, dependability, curiosity, charity, enthusiasm, empathy, excellence, flexibility, generosity, fun, honesty, growth, intelligence, leadership, kindness, innovation, humor, and honesty.

Find out which of the most common core values resonate with you. Create a list of your own core values, the ones that describe your most frequent behaviors and feelings correctly. With the help of the list, you will get to discover your core values, which can boost your confidence and ability to make the right decisions. By learning about your values, you get to choose an activity that can help the community and make you feel genuinely happy at the same time.

Think of people whom you admire

Identifying your values also often requires considering those who inspire you – the ones that you admire the most and keep on leaving a good impression on you. Note that a person's core values are often personified in those they love and admire. In most cases, the specific values you admire in others are also the ones that make up your personality.

Create a list of at least six people who receive your admiration. They should be role models or have valuable connections with you. For instance, write down the name of a colleague who you admire because of his commitment and perseverance. You may also put the name of someone who inspires you because of their naturally empathetic personality.

Include the names of those you consider heroes, too. An example would be Martin Luther King Jr. whose kindness is always imminent. He was also a fighter of social justice, so he is indeed worth admiring. Take note of the qualities, values, and traits that the people on your list embody.

Take your experiences into consideration

Do you know that you will also be able to learn about your core values by looking back at your experiences, specifically both the hardest and the happiest moments of your life? The reason is that such experiences can give you a clear idea of how you respond to certain situations.

Let's say you received an award for teaching. In that case, there is a high chance that leadership and offering encouragement to others are among the values that matter the most to you. Meanwhile, your painful experiences may have revealed that compassion and empathy are among your best qualities.

Group the listed values into related categories or groups

By now, you may already have a list of your values and beliefs. The next thing you should do is review your entries and find out how to group them into categories. Let's say you have inputted learning, personal development, and growth in your list. The three are strongly related, so you can put them in a single category. You can also group together other related values, like punctuality, reliability, and stability.

After categorizing your core values, select a word capable of representing a certain group/category. It is even a great idea to enclose the other listed values in the group in parenthesis after the word you have chosen to represent it. By doing that, you can provide more context to the primary values that correspond with you.

Select your top core values

You should also rank your top values based on importance. As each person is different, you can also expect everyone to have a different number of core values. However, it would be ideal to narrow down yours to just around five or ten. If your list gives you over ten entries, then it is advisable to ask yourself and reflect on the specific values that are truly valuable to your life.

To make it easier to narrow down your list, leave it for at least a day then go over them again to find the ones that really reflect you and determine whether their order or ranking is correct.

Finding Purpose Through Service / Mission

Once it is clear to you what your core values are, it will be a lot easier for you to identify ways to contribute to society in a way that you don't stray away from what you believe in. How you contribute to society and help the community should always be based on your core values.

Note that the world needs our help no matter how small or big. The world that we are talking about here may refer to humanity in its entirety, a small community that you believe in and where you are a part of, or any time and place in between. The needs of the world will greatly depend on the needs that those around you expressed or your own impressions.

A few examples of the needs of the world include clean water, volunteers for election day, home heating, improved training for the police, and skilled nursing. This specific area of Ikigai that requires you to get in touch with your community and offer help clearly connects with other human beings, as well as the different things you can do for them that go beyond your own needs.

Now, how can you find purpose through service or mission based on the practice of Ikigai? You can make that happen by using your own values to contribute to society. Here's how:

Shop local

One mission that you can focus your mind on is commit to being a local shopper. In other words, you should start appreciating what your locality offers and buy their products instead of going for imported goods. You may think that this can't have a major positive effect on the community but the contrary is actually happening.

If you mainly shop locally, then you are also investing your money in the community. Every time you spend your money on local shops, you also offer your help and support to the community in your locality and ensure that the money you invested stays in your neighborhood.

The same amount can then be immediately reinvested through other products and services. You can, therefore, expect this move to turn into a simple cycle, which benefits everyone and make them happy.

Take part in charity and fundraising events

If you want to give back to the community, then take note that your options do not just include donating money. You can also contribute other things, like your skills, effort, and time. Another way to give back is to sponsor or participate in charity and fundraising events.

Many non-profit organizations are constantly in search of people willing to volunteer their efforts and time for various causes. Doing these things will give you the chance to help many people in need. As much as possible, look for charity events in line with your core values and principles, so you will feel a lot happier and more contented, which is what you should be after if you want to live life based on Ikigai.

Volunteer

You can also volunteer your talents, energy, and skills for causes that matter a lot to you. The good news is that you have several options for volunteering just within your locality. For example, you are allowed to volunteer in hospitals, senior homes, food banks, youth groups, and animal shelters.

You may also start looking into non-profit organizations in your locality. This is easy as a quick search online can reveal several opportunities where you can volunteer your time and effort. If there is a specific organization or cause that you plan to help, it is easy to just reach out to them immediately.

You are also allowed to volunteer at a place of worship, especially if you consider yourself having a strong connection to your faith and religion. What's good about this is that it allows you to establish and strengthen relationships with other members, find new ways of helping others, and keep your community strong.

Mentorship

Do you know you can contribute to the community and society by grabbing mentorship opportunities? This allows you to share what you know to the world. A lot of people may be able to take full advantage of the skills, knowledge, and experience that you can share with them by mentoring them. You can even mentor those who are in your social circle or your colleagues who are in great need of your help and expertise.

If you have no specific idea about where you can mentor people, you may want to contact various NGOs nationwide. These organizations can connect you with people within your community who may take advantage of your knowledge. Be a good mentor and inspire them to be better versions of themselves.

Organize and facilitate cleanups

You can also contribute to improving the community you are in and give it a much better visual appeal by scheduling and facilitating a huge cleanup. If you are thinking of giving this a go, then you don't have to worry too much as you don't need a lot of things to do this. The only things you will need are rubber gloves, some garbage bags, recycling bags, and a few volunteers.

You also have to search for a place, which is greatly in need of help and care. Just in your community alone, you can find several messy streets, public parks, and beaches that can greatly benefit from some cleaning. This move may even end up inspiring the whole community to facilitate the same activity, eventually turning your local area into a place that is not only clean and tidy but also pleasurable to look at.

Find a job in your local community that truly resonates with you

Go for a job that is truly meaningful for you. Note that having a job is an incredible way to give back to the community or society both directly and indirectly. If you wish to get a job that can benefit the community directly, then go for one, which helps local infrastructure and people. For instance, you can get a job as a construction worker, public servant or government official, or firefighter.

In case you are already working and you are contented with your job, you can find ways to help the society or community through your employment location. All it takes is to look for opportunities to volunteer or facilitate public outreach.

Aligning with Global Needs

Your mission should not just end with serving those part of your local community. You will feel a lot happier and obtain a genuine sense of fulfillment and contentment, which is what you are after as you practice

Ikigai if you try to address global needs. In this case, you should try to observe and explore the needs of the world.

To reveal your real mission and use it for the practice of Ikigai, take time to reflect on issues that deeply touch your heart. You should then explore ways to offer help or make a contribution. Determine global needs, specifically those that matter a lot to you or have significant meaning.

Keep on asking yourself about the specific challenges or issues that you really want to solve. Also, try to find out how your vocation and passion can guide and support you as you try to solve such global issues. Align your actions and movements with your identified strengths, passions, and global needs.

Develop mindful resolutions and keep yourself involved only in those activities that are part of the mentioned aspirations. Also, try to find out if you can work on a job that is in line with your interests and skills while giving you a stable income that provides enough room for use in extending your help to others.

As you try to align with global needs, do not forget to keep on experimenting and observing, too. Never hesitate to try doing new and unfamiliar things. Do various activities, even those that you are not familiar with, and observe the kind of joy that it brings.

If you find them intimidating, begin with small steps. Try doing something new that also has low stakes. You can then move on to more complex endeavors that have higher stakes. Use this to keep on gaining knowledge, and experiencing and achieving growth.

One more thing that's so important in addressing global needs through your mission in Ikigai is to gather honest feedback. Communicate with those you really find trustworthy and ask for honest feedback regarding your skills as well as your contributions to the community and the world, as a whole. Who knows? Some of them may be able to give you valuable insights to guide you in your journey toward finding your mission and practicing Ikigai.

Lastly, be patient and persistent. Remember that it may take a bit of time to find your mission and your Ikigai but having enough patience and persistence can bring you favorable results soon. Remind yourself that this entire journey is all about self-discovery, so you don't have to move like it's a race. Take your time until you find all the major pillars of Ikigai, including your mission or what the world needs that you can fulfill, so you can finally live a life full of meaning.

CHAPTER 6

Balancing Vocation/Profession with Your Skills and Passion

Now, it's time to tackle the last major component of Ikigai, which is vocation/profession (what you can be paid for) and how you can make sure that you get to balance it with your skills and passion. Getting a job in a field that you are genuinely passionate about and truly matches your skills can give you a different kind of high. It can give you real happiness, making you feel like you have really found your Ikigai (sense of purpose).

However, it is also not a secret that finding a profession that pays you well or gives you financial freedom is extremely important. You have to, therefore, find the right balance between finding the right vocation/profession (what you can be paid for) and your skills and passion.

Exploring Career Paths

Picking the correct career path is one of the most vital decisions that can greatly affect your life. As much as possible, look for a career path, which is in line with your passion, skills, aspirations, and values. You have to understand yourself, explore different choices, hone essential skills, set goals, and embrace adaptability, so you can bring yourself closer to a rewarding and fulfilling career.

Proper career exploration should always be an essential step to take during your journey to finding the most fitting profession/vocation for you. It requires a complete understanding of the things you love the most and the areas where you excel; otherwise, you will end up having a career that only makes you feel empty, uninspired, and unfulfilled.

By exploring your career options, you can reveal your real talents and passions, resulting in a higher level of job satisfaction and professional happiness. In the next section, you will get to know a few tactics to research potential career paths and find the one that truly resonates with your unique personality and aspirations. Here they are:

Perform a self-assessment first

A proper self-assessment should be the first step you should take in exploring your career paths. Here, you will have to identify and reveal not only your strengths but also your weaknesses, as well as some areas that require improvement. By evaluating yourself, you will gain a full understanding of your present skillset. You also have to clarify the different areas of your work that provide you with the highest level of satisfaction and are in line with your unique values.

As you perform your self-evaluation, do not forget to uncover your personal interests and understand each one. You have to try getting to know more about yourself deeply. Reflect on what interests you the most, your motivators, and the values you prioritize the most.

Take into consideration your skills and strengths, too, including those where you naturally excel and those that you were just able to hone as time goes by. Learning about these specific areas of your life can give you valuable insights into the kind of work capable of bringing you the kind of satisfaction and fulfillment you are longing for, especially in terms of your professional life.

Learn more about the career paths that truly captured your interest

Research the organizational structure as well as the different departments in your chosen career field. Get familiar with each one. If you are making your own career plan, then make it a point to research the levels and opportunities for growth that you can access in your chosen new field. You may also want to gather insights from trusted friends and co-workers who went through a career advancement in a similar field, so you will know exactly what your potential pathways are.

Look back at your previous achievements and experiences

It was discussed in an earlier chapter of this book how your previous achievements and experiences can give valuable clues regarding the things you find enjoyable and where you excel. Think of the previous roles, tasks, and projects you have handled that gave you a sense of joy and accomplishment.

Factor in the skills you utilized in the mentioned experiences and the way they align with your principles, values, beliefs, and interests. By taking a look at your journey in the past, you get to reveal some important patterns and preferences capable of guiding you to a kind of career that has real significance to you.

Set clear goals

The goals you should set can either be short-term or long-term. Ensure that they are suitable for your aspirations and personal values, too. The goals and aspirations you set can guide you in determining the specific path or direction you intend your career or profession to take.

When setting long-term goals, don't forget to think of the place where you think you will see yourself eventually whether it is for personal or professional purposes. Think of the meaning of success for you and how it would most likely appear to you. Consider how certain achievements can give you a sense of real fulfillment and satisfaction.

As you draft and clarify both your short- and long-term goals, you also get the opportunity to make your own roadmap – one that can offer guidance in making career decisions and actions for a future that is in line with your skills and vision. You have a much better chance of getting a rewarding career. This is especially true if you were able to gather valuable insights that will surely guide and bring you closer to a fulfilling profession or career.

Learn more about different types of jobs and various industries

Research the different job roles and industries presented to you as this can help in obtaining a comprehensive understanding of any opportunity that is available for you. Research the work culture, growth prospects, and requirements of different industries so you can figure out the one that is in line with your goals and interests. As you do proper and thorough research, you get to narrow down your list of options and then focus on fields that truly reflect what you love and who you are.

Think of what you are good at

As you try to explore the right career path for you, it helps to consider the specific areas where you are good. It would be better to pick a path, which is in line with your natural skills, talents, and gifts. This could be the key to feeling more satisfied, engaged, and accomplished with your chosen line of work.

Create an inventory of your identified strengths and skills then list down prospective careers that let you take advantage of them. Let's say, you are good at organizing things. In that case, you may want to look for a job, which lets you utilize your organizational skills (ex. event planning). If you're so good at making delicious cakes and cheesecakes, then it's a great idea to explore a career path that involves baking.

Stop thinking about money for a while

Yes, you need to consider money and the earning potential of a prospective career before diving into it but you have to keep reminding yourself that money can never buy genuine happiness. This means that the salary or amount you will receive should not be the sole driving force as you decide on the career path to take.

To determine what can truly make you happy, ask yourself what it is you are willing to do without receiving anything in return in case money is not an issue. Will you be happy volunteering your effort and time doing it forever? If you answered yes, then the path you are taking is most likely the one for you. However, if you answered no, it is highly likely that you won't enjoy that type of career.

Distinguish a hobby from a profitable passion

This type of exploration may be of help in finding an activity that you will love and keep you engrossed – one that will make you light up and make your heart feel genuinely happy. Make sure that you also balance it out by reflecting on who can benefit from your hobby or your chosen career path.

Ask yourself who you think will pay for whatever you can offer based on your hobby or career path. You can actually contribute to society through your hobbies and passion and have a source of income at the same time but before you can do that, you also have to be realistic. Be real as you ask yourself whether your hobby or passion has the potential of turning into a flourishing career – money-wise.

If not, is there something you can do to make it profitable for you? The goal here is to find the right balance between being happy doing what you love and enjoying a steady flow of income for yourself and your family. In this case, doing your own extensive research can be a big help.

Consider this an important step involving some informational interviews and networking. Talk to those who have a similar passion as you, so you will know whether they are earning money from it, how they make that possible, and the other work, effort, and skills they have to put in to turn the same passion that they have into something profitable.

You may also want to look into free resources online that aim to guide you to a path, which has a plausible career around your specific interests. Let's say you are passionate about reading and writing. If that's the case, you are allowed to look into a list of jobs intended for those who are fond of using words.

It is also advisable to assess whether doing it for a living is something that you will enjoy. The reason is that there are those who are passionate about something but want to do it only for the sheer fun of it.

If you are one of them and you decide to turn your passion into work, then you may end up changing it from one that you genuinely love to do into an activity that you have to do, which can significantly reduce your excitement about it.

Achieving Work-life Balance

Balancing your profession with your passion and skills to attain the real purpose of Ikigai also requires you to work on achieving a proper work-life balance. This means that you should not only dedicate your time and effort to your chosen career but also have to live a life out of it. There should be a balance between your personal and professional life. This is the key to finding your real sense of self and purpose, ultimately giving you the happiness and satisfaction promised by regularly practicing Ikigai.

After choosing a career path based on the concept and principles of Ikigai, it is time to amplify its ability to give you real happiness and satisfaction by giving in to the demands of your career while still not forgetting your personal life. You can achieve such kind of balance by doing the following:

Practice proper time management

Proper time management requires you to identify your priorities. You have to know exactly what your priorities are. Note that your priorities will always be personal to you. The only one who can determine what you want to prioritize is you, so don't let other people or the norm dictate what you have to focus on – after all, it's your happiness that is at stake, which is what you should be after in your quest for your Ikigai.

So whether you want to put your work on top of your priorities since you are aiming for a promotion or reduce the time you spend answering emails after work, you should do it. Establish your boundaries and figure out how to manage your time more efficiently based on your unique priorities.

To manage your time well, you should review the way you spend it at present and find out whether you need to make some adjustments to your current schedule. If necessary, block your time so you can focus on just a single area at a particular time. You may also want to utilize the matrix system, which helps establish priorities every time some tasks pop up all of a sudden.

As you manage your time, make sure to focus on attaining a kind of balance that gives you genuine happiness and makes you feel healthy, instead of pressuring yourself to divide your time at work and home equally. Note that while there are those who feel fulfilled and satisfied if they work more hours, others experience more happiness if they spend more time at home.

With that, you should assess yourself and try to find the perfect balance while factoring in your professional and personal goals, income, and quality time. Your goal here is to organize and prioritize your tasks efficiently and make sure that you dedicate sufficient time for your responsibilities at work and your personal pursuits, like family time, doing your hobby, and going after your personal goals.

Set boundaries

Your work-life balance and time management skills will also greatly improve if you learn how to set boundaries. Nowadays, employees have the option to work remotely, thanks to the advancements in technology and the flexibility of some employers to adapt to changes.

The problem is that this option for remote work also causes difficulty in disconnecting personal and work time. With that said, you really have to learn how to set clear boundaries and strictly follow them. Avoid checking your email once you clocked out of work so you won't end up disrupting the time you set aside for yourself and your family.

It also helps to reduce the amount of time you spend on certain roles if necessary. Assess your different roles both in your personal and professional life and find out where you can deduct some time. It would be nice to monitor your time for around one to two weeks so you can understand where your daily minutes and hours go specifically.

After that, find out whether there are daily tasks you can delegate to others, like your colleagues, other professionals, your kids, or your partner or spouse. Determine if there are tasks you can completely skip, too. In addition, you have to identify the tasks where you think you can spend less time. That way, you can set your own boundaries and limitations and focus only on those tasks that specifically require your attention every day or those that truly matter.

Include your health in your priorities

If you have good emotional and physical health, both your personal and professional life will also become rewarding. You should, therefore, take simple yet sure steps to promote better health and well-being. Make it a point to eat a healthy diet, do regular exercises, and get a sufficient amount of sleep.

Do not forget to meditate, too. Doing all that can improve both your mental and physical health that can also lead to a higher level of productivity and motivation – both of which are also essential if you want to have a healthy and flourishing career.

Love your job

You need to find a job you truly love, which is why you have to delve deeper into your sense of purpose (Ikigai) and determine your passion. Being passionate about your chosen line of work will increase the likelihood of you feeling happy when you are in the workplace. This can boost your motivation, making you even more efficient in getting things done on time.

Take time to assess whether you love and enjoy your current position and field. If you don't like it, ask yourself what you intend to do instead. Think of the hobbies you truly love and the present experience and skills you consider transferrable. Find a means of transitioning to a job you will surely love.

Value your energy

You can also attain proper work-life balance if you make sure that you honor your energy. Remember that your attempt to build a life of fulfillment and satisfaction based on the concept of Ikigai also requires energy. However, you should remind yourself that you will only feel good and happy if you use your energy on really valuable roles and duties that matter to you.

To honor your energy, you should observe your body. Pay close attention to the way it responds to certain situations and responsibilities. Determine the time when your body feels more alert and fully prepared to handle responsibilities. Tackle significant tasks and responsibilities when you feel the most alert and energetic. Don't forget to rest whenever you feel like your energy is naturally dwindling.

Find out whether there are certain activities, habits, and even people that seem to drain your energy. Let's say, for example, you have this colleague who keeps on airing his complaints about his work to you. This may drain your energy and attract negative vibes. In that case, it would be much better if you avoid such a colleague or any other toxic person around you.

Spend your time on activities that give you positive energy, like listening to relaxing sounds that tend to boost your energy and inspire you. If you are still unsure what it is that drains your energy, you should spend one to two days jotting down your feelings and emotions during and after doing your everyday tasks and activities. Believe me, you can protect your time and energy, attain work-life balance, and finally discover your Ikigai if you try uncovering your own energy drains and learn how to avoid them.

CHAPTER 7

Ikigai in Different Contexts

Now that you are familiar with the major pillars of Ikigai, it is time to uncover how they specifically appear in different contexts of one's life. Note that the practice of this concept can truly make a hugely positive difference in various aspects of your life. By learning how it works in different contexts and areas of a person's life, you can easily take advantage of it and let it do its magic on you.

Ikigai in Personal Life and Relationships

If you think about what could give your life more meaning, which is what Ikigai is all about, your usual response is most likely your personal life and the relationship you build with your loved ones, especially your friends and family. The good news is that with Ikigai, you can have a more meaningful life through the connections and relationships you build.

In the context of your personal life, Ikigai plays a major role in increasing your happiness. As you live your life aligned with the Ikigai you discovered, you can expect all your daily activities to be filled with satisfaction and joy. This is made possible by the fact that you are finally living your life with a purpose. Such an alignment boosts your mood and gives you a more positive perspective on life.

Expect your stress level to go down, too. You are already probably aware of how stress can lead to dissatisfaction. You may even end up feeling disconnected from life. Since you have already discovered your Ikigai and worked on keeping it aligned with the things you truly love, your skills and talents, and the needs of your community and the world, you have a much better chance of enjoying life with less stress.

In addition, you will feel a sense of tranquility, calmness, and balance. You will feel more fulfilled since you are finally doing what you are passionate about while making positive contributions to the community and the world. With that, Ikigai will be on its way to enriching your life and those surrounding you.

Ikigai can also give your desired personal growth. Once you discover your Ikigai and live with it, expect to go through a positive journey that focuses on improving yourself. Basically, you will see yourself exploring new areas of interest, further resulting in you improving your talents and skills and broadening your horizons.

All these positive effects of Ikigai on your personal life can also work wonders on your personal relationships. The fact that you are now filled with positivity means that you can start building more meaningful connections with those around you, especially your family, friends, colleagues, and other people you trust. You get to strengthen your relationship with them, too.

As you now have a much broader perspective, expect to empathize and communicate with people better. This can, of course, give your life more meaning and purpose since you can now relate to people a lot more efficiently, boosting your chance of cultivating stronger and deeper relationships.

Ikigai in Health and Well-being

As far as your overall health and well-being is concerned, you can also count on your discovered Ikigai to be of help to you. By ensuring that your daily activities are in line with your own Ikigai, there is a low chance for you to experience stress. You will feel more at ease and relaxed instead.

The reason is that Ikigai is the key to releasing unwanted and negative emotions healthily. The fact that you are now pursuing what you are passionate about is an opportunity to practice self-care, which is also an effective stress management technique. Your mental health and overall well-being can, therefore, benefit greatly from Ikigai.

One more thing that Ikigai can do for you if you live your life by it is that it can make you stronger and more resilient. Your Ikigai is going to let you live a life with meaning and purpose, which will eventually increase your likelihood of enjoying a longer lifespan, better emotional and mental health, and lower risk of experiencing chronic illnesses.

Apart from its relaxation advantages, getting engaged in activities that showcase your creativity, such as sculpting, drawing, and painting, can benefit you physically, too. Let's say, for instance, you decide to make art. This particular activity can reduce the level of cortisol, a stress hormone, inside your body. What's great about having a low cortisol level is that it also lowers inflammation, a major contributor to certain diseases, like diabetes, arthritis, and heart disease.

Ikigai can indeed give you a form of self-care, which lowers your stress and boosts your mental and physical health. As you devote time doing your passion, you also get to focus on your well-being, resulting in you actively contributing to your own happiness and genuine fulfillment.

Ikigai and Spirituality

At the heart of Ikigai lies its deep connection with spirituality. Those who made Ikigai a part of their lives already witnessed first-hand how strongly connected this concept is to their spiritual beliefs. You may view it as just a simple means of identifying your purpose at first, but eventually, you will realize that it actually taps a lot of things on a much deeper level, including your connection to your inner self, to those around you, and the universe.

In the context of practicing Ikigai, it is safe to describe spirituality as your sense of connection to things larger than yourself. These could be the divine, nature, or collective awareness of humanity. So how do spirituality and Ikigai connect? Let's explore the reasons here.

Requires you to live in the now or present moment

A lot of spiritual and religious platforms focus on the significance of mindfulness and meditation. Several of them even encourage their proponents to practice the act of being completely present in the moment – the here and now. The same focus is what Ikigai inspires among its followers. The process of identifying your Ikigai requires you to pay attention to and prioritize your skills, passion, and influence and impact on the now. In other words, you have to savor your journey instead of solely focusing on your destination.

Serves a higher purpose

Most religious and spiritual traditions talk about how important it is to find meaning and value in service – one bigger than yourself. It is also what Ikigai will teach you to do. It inspires you to think of how you can contribute to your community and the entire world through your skills and passion. It is basically locating your spot in a large and wide web of life.

Encourages to practice a state of flow

Ikigai is applicable to spiritual practices in the sense that it also requires practitioners to create a state of flow. This refers to being deeply absorbed in the now (current moment) and enjoying it genuinely. This kind of flow is what both spirituality and Ikigai are after. Once you get fully engrossed in your discovered Ikigai, you will no longer be able to notice how much time you spent on it, especially if you also experience a high level of fulfillment.

Promotes appreciation and gratitude

Several spiritual platforms and paths have gratitude as their primary foundation. Once you become aware of your own Ikigai, you will also start genuinely appreciating your talents, skills, the opportunities around you, and the real happiness that life brings. Your gratefulness towards your Ikigai also deepens your life's meaning and purpose.

Helps you find balance and harmony

One important principle of those who practice Ikigai is that they should find balance and harmony in every aspect of their lives. This means that you should not just focus on your personal pursuits and career but also your spirituality or spiritual beliefs and practices. As you align your intentions and actions with your deep sense of spirituality and purpose, you will feel more fulfilled.

Guides you to live a life with intention

Another major resemblance between spirituality and Ikigai is that both have the main theme of living with purpose or intention. Basically, it requires you to choose the way you should live your life consciously and align all the things you do every day with your beliefs, principles, and values. You can expect a more purposeful and meaningful life that is harmonious with your real self if you live with intention as what Ikigai and your spirituality teach.

Ikigai in Professional Life

Fresh out of college, the first thing that may come across your mind is to look for a job that pays really well. After several years, though, you may end up like others in desperate search of a somewhat elusive work-life balance. Fortunately, Ikigai can make that attainable for anyone.

Note that truthfully, it is tricky to align your passion and what you love with the things you decide to do for a living. The reason is that your passion and desires do not necessarily equate with the things you are good at. Your skills and talents or the things you are good at do not also necessarily mean that you will immediately find a job related to those that pay well.

You may find these life incongruences overwhelming but those are truths so you have to do something to conquer them. The best thing that you can do is to separate or distinguish them. Fortunately, Ikigai can help you do that as it also plays a major role in your professional life.

Based on the four major pillars of Ikigai, it is safe to say that finding it also means that you will be on your way to getting the career you have been dreaming of. Imagine having a career that is also your passion, requires you to use your unique skills and talents, gives you a sufficient amount of money, and allows you to serve your community. It definitely feels like a dream.

The ultimate solution to making Ikigai work positively for you as far as your professional life is concerned is to find your calling. Note, though, that this is kind of tricky but with proper and careful discernment, you will really be able to unleash your calling. You may have heard some stories of really major changes in career with the primary goal of pursuing dreams. For instance, there are those who quit a high-paying corporate role to work on a job with a meager income all because they have finally unleashed their calling.

Your case does not have to be extremely drastic and tricky, though. You can still do what you love and earn what you think you deserve. The first thing to do is to consider the specific tasks and roles that you find the most pleasurable in your present job. For example, you should discern what you love the most – working in isolation or with a team. Do you prefer doing more technical tasks or general and administrative tasks?

The goal here is to really dig deeper within yourself and find out what your heart is telling you. You also need to sift out certain work areas you dislike and try to do more of those you love. By doing that, you can begin to unleash your Ikigai slowly and make it work for you in terms of your career.

Loving and Embracing the Entire Journey

Identifying your Ikigai and its benefits on your personal life, relationships, career, health and wellbeing, as well as your spirituality, can be a lifelong journey. The whole process should not just be perceived as a destination as it will always be a path and journey that you have to go through for a lifetime.

To make it easier to embrace the whole journey, you need introspection and perseverance. You also have to be willing to accept even those that are unknown and unfamiliar to you.

In addition, remember that throughout the process, expect to encounter some setbacks, struggles, and challenges, but you have to look at them as opportunities for learning and growth. You should embrace and accept the journey as only then can you expose yourself to new experiences and fresh opportunities that will dramatically improve your life.

CHAPTER 8

Living Your Ikigai

To live your Ikigai means you have to commit to being fully present. Be willing to live life a day at a time and make an honest effort, too. The premise behind the practice of Ikigai is that you should give your best in everything that you do in accordance with what you have while ensuring that you don't experience burnout. If you achieve that, then you can rest every night feeling genuinely fulfilled and happy.

Your Ikigai does not have to be the same as others. Anything that gives you a real reason for living can be considered your Ikigai, which is unique only to you. It could be a habit, an object, a person, or an event. Almost everything around you provided it gives your life meaning and purpose, is a source of Ikigai.

Once you have discovered your Ikigai, the next thing you ought to do is to make sure that you get to incorporate it into your daily life. Get to know how you can live your Ikigai every day in this chapter.

How to Incorporate Ikigai Practices into Your Daily Life?

As you may have known by now, the Japanese culture looks at Ikigai as the secret to living a happy and long life. The reason is that it requires you to compile the things that give you real joy and figure out some things you can do to serve a large part of the community or even the world.

Once you accomplish that, you can easily define what Ikigai means to you personally. But how can you really make Ikigai a part of your life and daily practices? Here are a few tips:

Begin small

After identifying and establishing your calling, start to tap into it slowly but surely. Begin small by creating daily, weekly, or monthly goals. It helps to take baby steps when trying to tap into the wonders of your Ikigai. For instance, your goal could be as trivial as starting the habit of journaling, taking a walk in the morning three times every week, or not checking your social media accounts for a specific number of hours in a day.

It could also be staying away from any form of distraction so you can optimize the hours you spend at work. Another seemingly trivial but extremely important goal you can try achieving every day is making it a daily habit of meditating for at least ten minutes. The premise here is to keep yourself grounded through routines. Focus on small details and positive actions (ex. waking up early or preparing a healthy meal).

Create a plan

Based on the small goals you identified, it would be helpful to organize them into short-term and long-term goals. Put them in a chart or notebook and put in a place where you can see right away so you can immediately look at them whenever necessary. You can even create monthly goals and then from there, you should make your daily and weekly goals.

Let's say, for instance, that you set a monthly goal of going through leadership development training. In that case, the first goal you should have for the week is to search for legitimate training programs. The second goal you can set for the week is to organize meetings online with prospective mentors.

Again, it is important to put your list of goals, whether short-term or long-term, in writing. Use a notebook, calendar, chart, or anything that will serve as a dedicated area for the plans you have set for yourself. Ensure that you can refer to them anytime. It is also advisable to have both a paper and digital copy of it, so you will still have a reference in case one of them goes missing. Put the paper copy in a visible place, like in the mirror of your bathroom or the bulletin board at your office.

Remain active and never retire

This is part of the major principles of Ikigai. You should keep yourself active and avoid retiring. Remember that if you give up on your passion and skills, then you may also end up losing your life purpose. With that said, it is crucial to continue doing valuable and meaningful things and see yourself making progress.

Never entertain the thought of quitting or retiring. Be active by doing many things that resonate with your passion, vocation, and mission. Provide utility or beauty to those around you, help out, and try to shape the world surrounding you the way you want to. Expect to witness life in a much different light, and a positive one at that, if you do such things.

Avoid excessively filling your stomach

In terms of eating for a healthy and long life, the less is more principle is applicable. Also, based on the 80-percent rule, staying healthy for a long time requires eating less than your hungry stomach demands rather than stuffing yourself. It is also a popular concept among the Japanese who believe that eating only up to eighty percent full can ensure that you stay healthy and prevent the need to visit the doctor regularly. Practice this every day and you will also feel more fulfilled, less guilty, and happier with your life.

Remain fit

This tip could be in relation to the one mentioned earlier about not stuffing yourself with food. You have to make it a point to stay in shape. If you have been out of shape for a while, then try to bring it back with your next birthday as your target date for reaching that goal.

Note that just like water that seems to be at its best if it does not stagnate and remains fresh, your body can also be expected to move more efficiently if you work on maintaining it every day. Your goal is to keep your body running for a long time. You can do that with proper daily exercise, which is also a good thing as it can release feel-good or happy hormones.

Smile everyday

Don't forget that your ultimate goal for practicing Ikigai is to prevent happiness from becoming so elusive. You can embrace real happiness by making it a habit to smile even when dealing with troubles. By nurturing a cheerful personality, you get to relax, stay happy, and make friends along the process.

Yes, there are times when you will be facing unfavorable situations and you have to embrace them, too but you should remember that in the practice of Ikigai, you should keep reminding yourself that it is a privilege to still be alive and present in the now. Waking up each day is always an opportunity for growth and to explore a wide world filled with many possibilities.

Connect with nature

This is another way for you to incorporate Ikigai into your daily living. Note that as humans, we are always a part of the world naturally. Even though most people are in the city nowadays, it is still crucial to recharge your battery by trying to connect with nature.

If you know shinrin-yoku, a Japanese word, then you are probably aware that it literally means forest bathing. It is a term used when you connect with nature with the help of all your senses, namely sense of taste, touch, smell, hearing, and sight. This is also a famous mindfulness practice in Japan and you can apply it in your attempt to embrace your Ikigai by reconnecting with nature. What's great about practicing this is that it can give your body the much-needed rejuvenation and your mind some peace.

Appreciate even those little things

You should find joy in the smallest of things. Appreciate and savor sensory pleasure, specifically those coming from the things that most people overlook and ignore. Consider how much effort or skill you apply in the things you do every day – after which, you should determine which of these daily activities evoke good and positive feelings so you can focus on doing them better and more often.

As much as possible, make it a habit to do such activities that imbibe positivity. Expect to feel more thankful and grateful for your skills and talents, as well as the things and people surrounding you if you do that.

Don't be afraid to rely on others

This can help you achieve the harmonious and sustainable nature of Ikigai. Never be afraid to ask for help and rely on others. You can make your life more pleasurable if you share and engage with other people by asking for help and offering it in return. Exert effort to communicate with and talk to people around you. Talk about both trivial and important topics.

Aside from your goals, you can tackle your passions, the simple things and pleasures in life, special moments you love and appreciate, and other stuff. Make an effort to build bonds among those part of your community. Try to absorb their positive energy and emit the same to them.

Dare to try new things

Each person is unique, so you can also experience and define your personal Ikigai differently. For example, you can find an introvert who makes Ikigai a part of their life by searching for a podcast that tackles and explores new experiences and ideas. With Ikigai, you will become even more familiar with yourself and have the confidence to explore new things and grab unique opportunities.

This will also give you moments wherein you feel like you have reached your desired state of flow. These are those instances when all things seem just right. In most cases, your Ikigai has to be in action so you can better define and determine what this concept is for you. You can make your Ikigai work by trying and experiencing new things.

Release yourself through acceptance

Another thing that you can do to embrace Ikigai and make it part of your daily life is to make it a habit to release yourself and you can do that through self-acceptance. Keep in mind that you can only successfully find and use your Ikigai if you truly understand the person you are and the things you believe in and stand for.

This does not necessarily mean it would be impossible for you, your actions, and your thoughts to change eventually. As a matter of fact, discovering your Ikigai also means that you should expect change from time to time. What's important here is to embrace who you are and accept yourself. Allow yourself to be just you no matter who it is.

Look for your own flow and balance

You can do that if you let yourself be in the now or the present moment. Exercise mindfulness of your own feelings as well as your environment. Use all your senses to appreciate everything you can then exert effort to get really attuned to your own life.

Your actions do not have to be grand as even simple ones can already help, like deep breathing, holding the breath for a while and slowly releasing it. This deep breathing activity is usually enough to bring your mind into its right frame. Expect to see things more clearly when doing this plus you will notice that your succeeding steps have become more grounded.

Beat procrastination

Your tendency to procrastinate could be a major obstacle in your attempt to achieve great results by making Ikigai a part of your life. Whether you are still beginning to do something or already have a clear direction or purpose, you will still have a hard time dealing with procrastination when it strikes.

Many procrastinate for a wide range of reasons – among which are fear of failure, a perfectionist attitude, and impatience. It could also be because you lack motivation. The problem with letting procrastination rule over you is that it prevents you from doing what you are supposed to do that's beneficial for you. You end up not doing anything to conquer the challenges and struggles you are supposed to overcome.

Instead of procrastinating, Ikigai encourages you to face your challenges and struggles head-on. You have to confront them; otherwise, you will never get the chance to reach for your goals and achieve success. You can choose to let yourself work diligently as a means of overcoming obstacles or pause completely (in that case, you can keep your steady pace and do nothing).

Note, though, that inaction has its own dangers. It can hurt and hamper your growth and development. You may even end up losing your interest in your passion or in finding your Ikigai. You may experience instant relief from pressure, anxiety, and stress if you decide to pause and stop taking action but this is just momentary. This kind of relief brought on by procrastinating is usually fleeting and illusory.

A brief pause can even result in huge consequences, including a stagnation period that is lengthier than necessary. Procrastinating for a long period can also result in a constant cycle of avoidance, which can undermine your ability and potential to attain success and discover your Ikigai. It is the deadliest disease that can have a huge and heavy toll on your happiness and success.

All the resources, effort, and time you invested in creating and preparing a plan will turn out to be a waste if you fall into the trap of procrastination and inactivity. Being aware of these negative effects of procrastination is a huge help if you want to take proactive measures that will bring you closer to your goals and your desired happiness and sense of purpose.

Take slow but sure steps

Making Ikigai a part of your daily life involves taking all necessary steps to achieve and find your Ikigai. While you can't avoid the tendency to procrastinate as it is a part of your journey, you should keep on reminding yourself that it will never lead you to a path of a productive and fulfilling life.

Pausing can give you instant relief from pressure but its detrimental effects in going after your passion outweigh it. With that said, you need to overcome not only procrastination but also other obstacles that may stop you from striving to reach your Ikigai.

The good news is that the beauty and magic of Ikigai can be seen in its ability to give you a chance to begin again, sometimes even repeatedly if needed. This means it lets you try several times or take several slow but sure steps until you reach your desired destination. Also, remind yourself that your past experience will serve as your guide and foundation for new attempts in the future. You can begin again from scratch as doing so is not actually a hindrance but an opportunity for growth and learning.

Find fulfillment through work

One important aspect associated with Ikigai is work. This means that the whole process of practicing Ikigai does not involve sitting idly. What you ought to do, instead, is to find fulfillment and satisfaction, a genuine one, through your work. This makes it different from the Western habit, which involves separating personal life and work. In Ikigai, you will be encouraged to incorporate your passion into your career or any professional endeavor.

Ikigai mainly requires you to keep your passion in line with your profession or vocation, making it possible for your present line of work to turn into a more enjoyable pursuit, which can significantly improve your well-being. Ikigai also knows how the body, spirit, and mind are so interconnected, which is the reason why its focus is on daily practices capable of nurturing each aspect of a person's being.

It could be your regular exercise or physical activity, attempts to eat mindfully, and daily spiritual reflection. Whatever it is, you can safely look into Ikigai as a way of prioritizing self-care designed to lead to a more fulfilling and balanced life.

CHAPTER 9

Overcoming Obstacles

Just like other concepts and practices that aim to give you your heart's desires and happiness, your journey toward discovering your Ikigai will also be filled with obstacles and challenges. Yes, it is the ultimate secret to finding your desired fulfillment and overcoming the challenges and obstacles you have in life, but there are also hindrances in your attempt to explore it and find your life purpose.

Basically, Ikigai requires you to discover the intersection between your passion, skills and talents, mission, and vocation. The sweet spot in this intersection, which is only unique to you, is what will give your life more meaning and help you attain satisfaction. This is why it is the Japanese term used to refer to one's purpose in life or reason for being. It is anything that inspires you to wake up each day, get up, and feel the excitement of tackling all the things you need to do for the day.

The journey will not be smooth sailing, though. Expect to encounter some humps as you start to uncover what your Ikigai is but as soon as you grasp your purpose clearly, you will be more equipped to deal with the challenges along the way.

Common Obstacles You Will Encounter

It is possible for you to find your Ikigai in your minor everyday rituals, small and deep conversations, as well as side projects. You can also search for it during moments of idleness and silence and in those instances when your creativity flows. Be prepared, though, as there are common obstacles you will most likely encounter during your quest for your Ikigai. Among the obstacles you have to prepare for and try to overcome are the following:

Uncertainty and fear

The most common challenges you will have to go through as you try to find your Ikigai are fear and uncertainty. Note that the whole process requires you to embrace the unfamiliar and venture into the unknown. Just thinking about the change that you will have to go through and the growth that may come along with it can result in uncertainty and fear, especially if you are still unsure how to deal with it.

If this is what's going inside your mind right now as you try to identify your Ikigai, you should remember that it is actually natural for you to feel afraid and uncertain. Naturally, it is how you respond to things and activities that require you to go out of your comfort zone. Fear is even a good thing as it indicates that you are embarking on something vital and significant.

The only thing you have to do is to embrace the discomfort, rather than avoid it, and think of it as a sign that you are on your way to widening your horizon and stretching your boundaries. Perceive the feeling of being afraid as your compass that guides you to achieving growth – whether in your personal or professional life.

Never let this feeling paralyze you. What you should do instead is channel it so it will serve as your inspiration and motivation. If you are still afraid, then it would be a great idea to imagine the happiness and exhilaration that you will most likely feel once you conquer your fear and the challenges that come your way and allow yourself to push your limits. The goal here is to perceive fear as empowering, so it will turn out to be your catalyst for growth, instead of a huge hindrance or obstacle.

Lack of patience and persistence

Again, you will not be able to find your Ikigai immediately. As a matter of fact, the journey will most likely be long and somewhat never-ending. You have to navigate through this journey with patience and persistence; otherwise, you will not be successful in identifying your Ikigai.

To somewhat encourage persistence and patience during your journey, remind yourself that the path to Ikigai should never be perceived as a marathon or sprint. You need to spend time and practice dedication to reach the goals that are in line with your passion, vocation, profession, and mission. If you are not patient enough, then you may only derail any progress you have because of burnout and frustration.

Finding your Ikigai always translates to the need for cultivating patience. Accept the fact that it is impossible to attain meaningful goals and pursuits overnight. You can never rush it. Encourage patience by breaking down major and big milestones into smaller ones you can easily and quickly achieve.

Every step you take while moving forward, even the most trivial ones, is the ultimate secret to reaching your Ikigai. Make sure that you reward yourself for even these small wins and victories since these show proof of your progress and dedication to be successful.

Also, keep in mind that the key to success will always be your persistence. Once you see setbacks and challenges arising, remember the reasons why you decided to pursue goals aligned with your Ikigai. Accept setbacks and look at them as opportunities for growth and learning instead of being signs of failure. Hone your resilience and make sure to have a steady space, which will be the key to navigating all the twists and turns you will encounter throughout your journey.

Fear of failure

Your fear of stepping out of your comfort zone and experiencing failure along the process could be the reason why there are several instances when you doubt your ability to find your Ikigai and attain your desired happiness and success from it. Since you are afraid to fail, you may end up stopping yourself during your pursuit of Ikigai.

If this kind of fear seems to be stopping you, it is time to remind yourself that it is actually alright to take small but sure steps. Even gradual changes matter. You may need to be really courageous and persistent as you try to overcome this fear but once you find your Ikigai and live your life with it, you will realize that the rewards are all worth it.

Cultural and societal pressures

Another possible hindrance in your attempt to find your Ikigai is the presence of external pressures and distractions. It could be from the pressures brought on by your culture and the society you are in. In most cases, what society believes in dictates the perception of people on success. This can cause conflicts and challenges when you are searching for your Ikigai.

To prevent that from happening, you should remain true to your values and your own personality. This means you have to stick to what you believe in even if it is unpopular when you consider the norm in society.

Avoid pressuring yourself too much from the external expectations of your culture, friends, and family. What you need to do, instead, is build your inner strength and clearly understand your goals and values so you can stay committed to your Ikigai.

Vagueness or unclear Ikigai

You may find it challenging and tricky to determine what your Ikigai is exactly. This is especially true if your own strengths and passions are still not clear to you. Don't feel frustrated if that happens. What you should do, instead, is allow yourself to reflect and explore for quite some time. As much as possible, look for reliable coaches or mentors who can guide you.

Participate in tasks and activities that make you feel curious and happy. Observe yourself when doing so since this will help you determine what it is that specifically energizes and excites you. Soon enough, with your openness to discover yourself and your patience, you will get a clear view of what you really want.

Effective Tips and Strategies to Build Resilience and Mental Toughness

Your Ikigai and your ability to be resilient even during the toughest of times are actually interconnected. The reason is that finding your real purpose or Ikigai requires you to be really resilient. You have to be tough both mentally and emotionally – after all, the whole journey will be filled with both ups and downs plus you will most likely encounter a lot of challenges and hindrances.

If you think about the act of finding your purpose, you may look at it as a really positive thing (which is the truth, actually). However, your sense of purpose won't come to you in just a snap of a finger. Your identified purpose can't also be expected to solve everything for you on its own. You also have to exert an effort to make it work in your favor despite the challenges associated with searching for it.

Keep in mind that there may be times when you will feel too overwhelmed with the process and frustrated because you feel like you are always a few steps behind. You may even come to the point wherein your purpose would be just getting through the day. It seems like prioritizing what truly gives you happiness is just a distant and unreachable dream.

This won't be the case if you get to unleash your inner strength, resilience, and mental toughness as you search for your Ikigai. If you are struggling right now, then your acquired resilience will serve as an effective means of enhancing your resilience and deepening your experience of it.

So how do you build your resilience and mental toughness so they can be of help in searching Ikigai? Here are a few techniques:

Practice mindfulness

Of course, this is one of the most crucial steps in building your mental toughness and resilience as it involves being completely engaged and present with the now, regardless of what you are doing, without any judgment or distraction. You can do a few mindfulness practices, like deep breathing, mindful walking, and meditation regularly to improve your focus and emotional control or regulation and lessen stress.

Be compassionate with yourself

Cultivating resilience and mental toughness to bring you closer to finding your Ikigai does not mean you should be hard on yourself. Make sure that you give yourself proper treatment. Be as kind and understanding to yourself as when you are with your closest friend.

Acknowledge the fact that you are struggling, especially in your quest for your Ikigai. Ensure that you also give yourself forgiveness for all the mistakes you have made. Embrace the truth that you are human; thus, you are subject to imperfection. By being more compassionate with yourself, you can boost your mental strength and fortitude, as well as your resilience, a key to familiarizing yourself with your Ikigai.

Go beyond your comfort zone

Never feel contented about being in just a steady pace. Do something different – one that is not within your level of comfort. Try new things and activities. Conquer your fears and make it a regular habit to challenge yourself. You can do this by beginning a new hobby, accepting a project that is challenging for you, and public speaking, Every time you allow yourself to go beyond your limits and step away from what is comfortable for you, you also get to cultivate your mental strength, resilience, and confidence.

Scrutinize the challenge

If you experience any of the challenges indicated a while ago during your quest for Ikigai, then it helps to learn how you can assess each one. For instance, if you are dealing with a challenge, take a pause and then practice deep breathing. After that, ask yourself and reflect on whether or not this challenge is a real catastrophe or just a mere inconvenience.

Note that there are several instances when people perceive even minor inconveniences as catastrophes. You have to distinguish the two as doing so can also guide you in boosting your resilience and making yourself more mentally tough. If what you are experiencing is just an inconvenience, it is possible to begin solving the problem. You can even brainstorm for ideas to solve it.

Also, take a look back at those instances in your life when you were able to use your problem-solving skills successfully. You may be able to apply it in your current situation, building up your resilience and mental strength.

Acknowledge your feelings

Even in those instances when you feel weak and doubtful as you are trying to discover your Ikigai, you should still acknowledge the presence of such feelings and process them. Understand your emotions completely, especially during tough and difficult moments.

To process your feelings well, you can try journaling. It is an effective means of processing your emotions. By putting your fears, thoughts, frustrations, and the things you are grateful for in writing, you have a much better chance of boosting your emotional intelligence, which is also an important aspect of resilience and mental strength.

Maintain a balanced point-of-view

As you face challenges during the practice of Ikigai, you should keep on reminding yourself of your long-term and short-term goals, as well as the bigger picture of practicing the popular Japanese concept. By doing that, you can prevent any temporary setback from overwhelming you and making you feel frustrated and doubtful. What's great about having a more balanced point-of-view is that it can also hone your perseverance and patience.

Cultivate meaningful connections

Another thing that you can do to make yourself more mentally tough and resilient is to establish meaningful connections and relationships. You will become even stronger mentally if you let yourself be in supportive and strong relationships with other people. With that said, it would be a good idea to surround yourself with those who know exactly how to uplift, motivate and encourage you. It is also a good idea to work for mentors or take part in groups that let you learn from them. As much as possible, look for those whom you can truly guide you.

Cultivate a positive mindset

Your goal is to build a more realistic and optimistic outlook in life, so you can clearly find your Ikigai or sense of purpose. To make that happen, you should practice positive self-talk. Make it a point to challenge your negative thoughts, too. By doing that, you can approach your life in a way that you solve problems instead of going away from them.

Adapt to change

Aside from the mentioned tips, you should also work on honing your ability to adapt to change. Remember that there are several changes you may encounter as you search for your Ikigai, so it is necessary to learn how to adapt. Embrace growth and flexibility and try to learn from your mistakes, failures, and setbacks.

Knowledge about these crucial points will help you look at these seemingly negative traits as opportunities for growth and learning. Rather than dwelling on the things you did wrong, it helps to go back to what you experienced and analyze it.

Learn about the four important Cs of mental toughness and resilience

If you are still unfamiliar with these 4Cs, then take note that it means confidence, control, challenge, and commitment. Basically, to be mentally tough and resilient requires you to hone your confidence, which is your ability to trust and believe in yourself and what you can do.

You also need to have proper control as you start searching for your Ikigai. Control, in the context of finding your Ikigai, involves managing your feelings and believing and understanding that you have full control and influence over your own life.

Commitment is another secret to building mental toughness and resilience as it lets you stick to tasks while perceiving them through completion. There is also challenge, which requires you to view changes and hardships as opportunities instead of threats. If you focus on these four Cs or areas of mental toughness, you get to build your resilience that will play an important role in your quest for your Ikigai and genuine happiness.

What Can Having Mental Toughness Do for You?

Being truly mentally tough means that you are capable of emerging stronger from difficult and challenging situations and experiences. Mental toughness encompasses your resilience, emotional intelligence, positive attitude, and ability to stay calm and focused even when dealing with pressure.

Developing real mental toughness that will help you deal with the major obstacles of identifying your Ikigai also helps you develop adaptability. In addition, this strong mental trait will encourage you to learn from your experiences and stop yourself from being too afraid of going beyond your comfort zone.

Debunking A Couple of Ikigai Misconceptions and Myths

As you develop your mental toughness and resilience and enjoy the benefits of having this mental strength, it is crucial to also learn about a few myths and misconceptions surrounding Ikigai. This is necessary for further improving your ability to handle the challenges associated with the practice of Ikigai.

Once you become aware of these misconceptions and the truths behind them, you can easily navigate your path to living with and discovering your Ikigai with a high level of confidence. You will also become more resilient as you seek purpose and genuine joy in your life's daily moments.

Ikigai is only essential for your career

This is a myth as finding your Ikigai does not solely revolve around landing your dream job. It goes beyond your career or profession. The goal of Ikigai is universal. It is about letting you gain fulfillment in various aspects of your life, even when it comes to your hobbies and personal relationships.

It aims to give people a more fulfilling life, which encompasses different areas, like personal growth, relationships, and even health. Expect Ikigai to integrate all these essential elements together, so you can enjoy a more meaningful and balanced life.

Your Ikigai will never change

The truth is there is a great possibility for the Ikigai you discovered now to change eventually as you can't expect it to be set in stone. Note that since humans go through growth and evolve along the process, it is also highly likely that their interests and passions will change.

With that said, it is advisable to revisit and redefine your Ikigai from time to time. Keep in mind that just like how dynamic life is, you are also prone to changing. Be willing to accept change and perceive it as a vital part of your entire journey. You need to make it a habit to revisit your Ikigai as it is the key to making it stay relevant for you and keep it aligned with the real you.

You should figure it all out immediately

No, there is no need for you to figure everything out right after you discover your Ikigai. Remind yourself that knowing your Ikigai is never a destination. It is a lifelong journey, so do not beat yourself up if you keep on being a work in progress. What you ought to do, instead, is embrace your unique journey and process. Be willing to discover yourself. Never aim to be perfect but work on achieving progress little by little.

Make sure that you also celebrate even small wins. If you committed mistakes along the process, learn from them. Note that pursuing your Ikigai revolves around continuous self-improvement and growth instead of getting to a final destination or endpoint.

CHAPTER 10

Sustaining your Ikigai

Ikigai puts a lot of emphasis on achieving growth through meaningful connections, mastery, and of course, your real passion. As you focus on the things that you truly love and the areas where you excel, you can continuously learn and improve along the process.

Make sure that you sustain your love and commitment to your Ikigai, though; otherwise, your progress and all your efforts will go down the drain. The journey should be continuous. It should be lifelong and should let you learn and grow all the time. This can help boost your resilience even further and equip you with the necessary skills to handle unexpected situations.

How Can You Sustain Your Ikigai (Sense of Purpose)?

Once you have already identified your sense of purpose (Ikigai), it is time to exert an effort to sustain it. Your goal is to keep inspiring yourself so you will not end up straying away. You have to continue living with your sense of purpose to continue enjoying its benefits and living your life with meaning.

Develop the habit of taking a mindful pause

As you may have discovered right now, mindfulness serves as a truly powerful instrument for reconnecting with the now. An effective way of practicing mindfulness every day is to spend a few minutes pausing whatever it is you are doing and instead, focus on breathing. Ensure that you are fully aware of your breath.

Observe your body's sensations while taking several deep and slow breaths. By doing this, you can boost your awareness of your emotional and mental state, thereby providing you with the means to respond appropriately, instead of reacting unnecessarily.

Reconnect with your Ikigai or sense of purpose

Do not let yourself lose your connection with your identified sense of purpose, so you can keep on living with it and not lose track of what life truly means to you. Whenever your mind has a bit of space, ask yourself and reflect on how you can be the best version of yourself.

Find out how you can connect each moment with a superior sense of purpose. It could be that you wish to leave a legacy in the world by making it a bit better than when you first stepped on it. It could also be that you wish to offer your kindness to the world or show more of your integrity and creativity.

What you have to focus on here is to continue linking the present moment with anything that inspires you and has real meaning for you. Perceive this as a playful and light exploration that you should do regularly instead of an intense soul-searching activity.

Be open to continuous exploration and growth and reflect and reassess yourself, so you will immediately notice if there are some changes in your sense of purpose (Ikigai). That way, you can make the necessary adjustments and keep on living the life you have dreamed of.

Learn ways for continuous growth and learning

To live a more meaningful life and ensure that you don't stray away from your Ikigai, you have to learn a few ways to learn and grow continuously. If you take the time and exert some effort in expanding your skills and mind through continuous learning, you will surely be able to achieve your goal of living and enjoying a more meaningful life.

You get to see new ways of thinking and opportunities capable of improving your life in different ways. Here are the things you can do for your continuous growth and learning:

- **Update yourself regarding your passions** – From time to time, you have to ask yourself whether the skills or topics that excite, interest, and energize you before still do the same for you right now. Keep in mind that there are several instances when your passion and sense of purpose change as you also grow and evolve. Take time to pursue your real passion and interest and make sure it is current. Doing what you truly love will make your life more fulfilling and meaningful.

- **Keep on challenging yourself** – Avoid setting into a routine that does not allow you to learn or improve. It always helps to go beyond what you are comfortable doing. Tackle new responsibilities and challenges as much as possible. By trying difficult and new things, you can definitely work out your brain and improve your resilience. You can only expect growth to happen if you continue pushing yourself out of your limits.

- **Mentor others** – You can also promote continuous learning within yourself and make you fall in love with your present sense of purpose even more if you teach or mentor others. Based on your skills, talents, and your real passion, you should mentor anyone who needs your guidance. You can also volunteer and spend time helping people within the community.

  What's great about mentoring others is that you get to explain concepts and share information in the area you are truly knowledgeable about, which is such an incredible learning experience. It also helps you gather new insights plus your understanding about your field of interest will become even stronger.

- **Remain curious** – Open up your mind and practice curiosity as you go through each day. Instead of letting things be, try questioning them. Be in awe of the world surrounding you and why things happen the way they do. Your curious mind should also encourage you to read books that tackle topics that you are not familiar with. If possible, go on trips from time to time so you get to immerse yourself in various cultures. Continuous learning is also possible if you constantly get curious and become thirsty for knowledge.

To ensure that you get to sustain your Ikigai, it is definitely a great idea to develop the habit of nonstop learning. It should be something that you do regularly not just during rare moments. It should be part of your everyday routine.

Start reading books, participating in discussions, taking online courses, and reflecting on things you have experienced so far. You should also take the time to review ways to improve yourself. By committing to experience constant growth and progress, your life will be filled with meaning, which is the key to non-stop learning.

Be willing to make sacrifices when necessary

Remind yourself that even if you have already discovered your Ikigai and you have finally started living a life with purpose, you are still not immune to sacrifices. Every now and then, you will need to sacrifice and give up something. Understand this fact and take this to heart so you won't end up getting frustrated and disheartened, resulting in being unable to sustain your Ikigai.

The goal here is to prepare yourself to make sacrifices when necessary to preserve your beliefs and values. This can help a lot in living a more purposeful and meaningful life. Commit to making some changes in your overall personality and attitude, if necessary, in case you are the type who can't seem to sacrifice anything right now.

Look for things capable of renewing your enthusiasm

No matter what your current circumstance is, your enthusiasm and energy will be the ones that will keep your fire burning. With that said, you really have to look for things capable of fueling your passion and sense of purpose. This is another case of self-discovery since you will be uncovering what truly makes you fulfilled and happy. By learning about these things, you can always renew your enthusiasm, thereby preventing you from losing track of your Ikigai.

Learn from failures and mistakes

Experience is always the best teacher, so if you commit mistakes and experience failures during your journey toward finding and sustaining your Ikigai, then avoid beating yourself up. You should learn from them instead of letting your frustration and discouragement rule over you. Nurture positive emotions, such as respect and gratitude instead.

Never feel guilty about failing and committing mistakes, too. Remember that your guilt is just going to hold you back from reaching your goals. Every time you feel extremely guilty, address it right away. Tell yourself that your failures are nothing to be ashamed of and feel guilty of. Throw your guilt and your disappointments out of the window so you can sustain your Ikigai and continue living a purposeful and meaningful life.

Cultivate connections

You will also feel more inspired to continue living with your discovered purpose if you keep on fostering and cultivating connections with others, especially those around you and who matter a lot to you. You can encourage a sense of togetherness and community if you continue to share your passion and participate in deep and meaningful conversations.

Establish a connection with others using not only your goals in life but also your simple and small joys. Build common bonds. It also helps to look for an accountability partner – one whom you can share your journey with. Take part in the activities in your community, too. Do not isolate yourself.

Through your active participation in the activities in your community, you get to build connections with those around you. You also get to absorb and reciprocate their positive energy. You should also try to be mindful of how social connections can affect your well-being and your ability to sustain your love for your sense of purpose.

Find sustainability and harmony

Note that the Ikigai philosophy has one major focal point it considers as extremely important – that is striving for harmony and balance in your life by giving both the society and nature respect. Think of your natural and social environment and whether or not it is sustainable.

Recognize the fact that if you also sustain your Ikigai, then it will also serve as an effective motivational force capable of aligning your actions and the steps you take with a higher and better purpose. This can result in you enjoying more harmonious surroundings that can give you peace and pure bliss.

Create a purpose timeline

It is highly likely for your purpose to change over time. It could be because as you age and gain more experience, your point of view on things also changes. Make it a habit to reassess and realign your sense of purpose with yourself. Think of the exact change that happened in your sense of purpose at various points in your life. The focus of the change should be periods of transition and evolution. Find out whether there are lessons here that apply to your present situation.

Think of the challenges and obstacles you have already gone through and successfully surpassed. Find out whether you can offer your help to those who experienced the same thing. That way, you will feel more inspired and keep on enjoying a life with meaning and purpose.

Nurture the attitude of gratitude

You should develop the habit of being thankful and appreciative of all the blessings you receive in life no matter how small or big. Do not forget to say thank you whenever you receive something. As much as possible, you should write down the things that you are thankful for every day in your gratitude journal.

Just seeing and reading the entries in your gratitude journal will be so inspiring and encouraging that even during tough and difficult days, you can expect your spirit to be lifted. When this happens, you will no longer find yourself straying away from your sense of purpose and feeling demotivated.

Celebrate achievements

To harness your sense of purpose and make sure that it continues to stick with you, you have to assess your milestones, progress, and achievements every now and then. Let yourself celebrate all these achievements. Even if it is just a small win, do not fail to pat yourself on the back. Keep track of your progress as it will surely give you the boost to persevere and sustain your love for your chosen Ikigai.

Prioritize your health

You can also prevent your motivation and your love for your sense of purpose from waning if you focus on caring for various aspects of your health, including your physical, emotional, and mental health. Your health should be on top of your priority, so you can live a more meaningful life and build the foundation to reach for your goals and create a difference.

Give your physical health a boost by starting to consume nutritious foods, getting enough sleep, and exercising regularly. Stay away from unhealthy vices and habits, too. Keep in mind that your physical health influences your mood and energy as well as your ability to deal with certain challenges in life. Choose to do things capable of strengthening your body and improving your resilience.

Your mental health should also be given priority. Keep in mind that the human mind is an extremely powerful tool, which makes it necessary to maintain its sharpness through reading, participating in debates and intelligent discussions, acquiring new skills, and finding solutions to complex problems.

If necessary, seek therapy or counseling to improve your mental health. Do not forget to recharge and relax, too. The current state of your mental health has a huge influence on your relationships, perspectives, and ability to do meaningful work, so you have to work on giving it a boost.

Your emotional health needs some attention, too. You can give this area of your health the care and attention it needs by indulging in self-care practices, nurturing your close relationships, and setting boundaries. Start expressing your gratitude, compassion, and love to those around you whenever possible.

Expect a huge and positive improvement in your emotional health by looking for genuine fulfillment and satisfaction from doing simple acts of generosity and kindness. By improving your emotional health, you can make yourself more capable of finding meaning and purpose and overcoming struggles.

Purpose and meaning always result from aligning your life with your main priorities and deepest values. Use your health as the foundation for it, enabling you to utilize your skills, gifts, and talents to serve not only yourself but also those around you in your own little way. Also, remember the profound connection of your body, mind, and spirit, so it is really a good idea to take care of yourself and your overall health holistically.

Being healthy here does not only mean that diseases are not present. It also means having sufficient energy, vitality, and a general sense of wellness. Include your health in your list of priorities every day and you will notice yourself starting to live a more meaningful and fuller life while keeping your identified sense of purpose or Ikigai sustained.

CHAPTER 11

Ikigai in Different Life Stages

Learning about Ikigai can benefit you no matter what stage of life you are presently in. It would even be better if you already applied this Japanese concept when you were still young or in your teenage years. This can help you take advantage of its positive effects on your life at an early age. Through Ikigai, you can reinforce the role played by a sense of purpose in your life, so familiarizing yourself with it early can be the secret to your success.

Ikigai for the Youth, Teenagers, and Early Adults

One thing about Ikigai is that it has a positive impact on the lives of the youth and teens in case they decide to make the concept a part of their lives. The fact that the goal of Ikigai is to provide one with a reason for living or a real sense of purpose means that it can keep the young ones going.

If you probe at the concept deeper, you will realize that it is a process of self-reflection. By knowing and understanding your Ikigai, you also get to understand yourself and your own beliefs and values even at a young age. It will also let you uncover the things that serve you once you are in the real and actual world.

The youth, teenagers, and early adults can even incorporate the Ikigai framework into their learning process, which is a huge help in boosting their focus, momentum, and motivation. Basically, it can open a pathway leading to their unique and individual purpose.

If you are still part of the youth, then Ikigai can define your life during your teenage years and answer an important question you often ask yourself – that is what is really your reason for living? Remember that you are not alone in wondering the answer to that question. A lot of teens and young learners also have a lot of questions regarding their sense of purpose.

It could be in the form of what they should do in a particular situation, what they should study next, what they want to become in the future, and the specific passions and interests they wish to explore. By learning about Ikigai, young learners like you will get the chance to shape your motives. The concept can also guide you in finding your real passion.

It serves as your means of identifying the why behind each action and thinking of what can give you joy and happiness now and in the future. Aside from helping you gain clarity in your vision, you also get to develop better mental and emotional benefits through it. As a learner, you will be guided through an Ikigai process driven and inspired by purpose. The reason is you will be required to consider what you love, your potential professional talents and personal skills, the needs of the world that you can most likely help, and the specific areas where you may be able to gain recognition.

As you keep on using Ikigai, you will gain a much deeper and profound understanding of yourself even if you are still young. With that, you can sharpen your ability to make decisions and ensure that they will always be based on what you find enjoyable and where you think you can apply your efforts based on your own talents and skills. You will also be able to grab opportunities leading to genuine self-fulfillment.

How to Practice Ikigai at an Early Age?

During your teenage or early adult age, you will most likely see your life being filled with emotions, confusions, curveballs, excitement, and impulsive decisions. This is the stage in your life when you are still confused as to what's the best career path for you or what your purpose really is. If you are not careful, you may end up following and pursuing unrealistic passions blindly and getting frustrated and discouraged upon seeing that your dreams do not seem to materialize the way you want them to.

This could be why others end up having a career that provides them status and a stable income but not real fulfillment and joy. This is the mistake you should attempt to avoid by practicing Ikigai when you are still young. That way, you will really land a job that truly resonates with your passion and gives you real happiness.

So now, how can you use Ikigai to make that possible? The first thing to do is to begin the journey by reflecting on your answers to the following important questions:

- What do you consider your best day? What does it look like? – Find out what encompasses a perfect day for you, one that gives you real and lasting happiness.

- What do you think are the things that keep you stagnant? Are there fears, doubts, or insecurities that keep you from moving forward?

- What are the things that you find easy to do? – These are the things that you truly enjoy doing that most times, you no longer notice the time passing by.

- Who are you usually with whenever you are alone? – You can answer this question honestly by tapping into your real inner self.

- How can you offer your help to someone? – Find out if there is something you can offer to someone that also gives you genuine happiness. Teenagers or young adults have a high chance of enjoying a better self-esteem after they offer their help to others, especially strangers, and volunteer.

For youth, the questions may be too deep or philosophical to answer. However, answering them honestly is a huge help in finding your passion and calling. The reason is that Ikigai for the youth, teenagers, and young adults is capable of addressing what is happening inside them, including their inner crises and confusions. It nudges them gently to reach their goals. By asking yourself such questions early, you can start building a solid foundation that will guide you to finding what truly matters to you, especially in terms of your career and personal life.

Middle Age and Finding Renewed Purpose

Ikigai can also help you live life with a meaningful purpose once you reach middle age. Note that once you reach this stage, there are moments when your motivation wanes. Unlike when you were still young, active, and inspired to do things, being in middle age may become the time when you will start questioning your purpose. This is possible if there are several goals and dreams that you have not able to fulfill yet.

If you keep on living your life based on the Ikigai concept, though, you can prevent your love for doing things from waning. As you try to live a life driven by purpose, you can expect to enjoy inner clarity and personal satisfaction. You get to prevent burnout and enjoy a meaningful life that's in line with your real passions.

While Ikigai works for all ages, it is particularly helpful for those in the middle age who already have more diverse experiences in life and work. The diversity of your experiences further increases your chance of getting pointed to the correct Ikigai.

Make an inventory of your skills, past and present jobs, etc.

Once you hit 40, expect to be greeted by a lot of realizations regarding yourself. You may look at this moment as the ideal form of crisis since it may bring you closer to your Ikigai. If you look back at all the years you have been living, you may realize that you have already held plenty of jobs. If you do, then you may start questioning yourself whether every job you had was just random or did each one brought you closer to your real Ikigai or sense of purpose.

To guide you to your Ikigai at this age, you should create an inventory of your skills, as well as all your previous employment. List down all the jobs you had throughout the years. It would even be ideal to include any side project or hobby you had in the past because each one uses your knowledge and collateral skills.

Once you have the list of activities, form two columns (similar to how you do a list of pros and cons). Rather than using pros and cons for the columns, though, you should think of a specific activity and the skills you used for it. You can use any term you want in every column, provided that it matters and makes sense to you.

When doing this activity, remind yourself that the result should not look like a resume. What you will be doing is a personal inventory – the one that resonates with you. Since it is unique to you and intended for personal use, do not hesitate to include skills not part of your job description.

The emotional part of this activity happens once you are in the stage of deciding on what particular column you will put each skill – the plus or the minus. In this case, it helps to visualize the position you have been dreaming of. You should then look at your list. Ask yourself whether the particular skill listed in each column will be included in the description of your dream job. If you answered yes to a skill, even during those moments when it's vague, you have to enter it in the plus column. Meanwhile, put the skills where you answered no in the minus column.

Remind yourself that this activity revolves around your emotional response, not your skill's actual proficiency. This is why there are cases when skills where you find yourself being highly proficient fall under the minus column while those used only a bit falls under the plus column. The segregation of your skills will always be dependent upon your present feeling.

The result of this inventory will definitely help you renew your sense of purpose as you hit middle age. It promotes self-realization, which can further enhance your eagerness to live. The reason is that you gain a more profound and deeper understanding of yourself, which encourages you to live and embrace life to the fullest.

You can also bring back or restore your sense of fulfillment as you go through your daily life. It lets you enjoy your everyday life's simple experiences and joys, leading to you appreciating and recognizing the fulfillment brought by those.

Once you hit middle age, you may also be looking for more motivation and inspiration to live. In that case, your Ikigai will serve as your driving force to continue propelling forward. With that, you can cultivate a kind of motivation and sense of purpose that will let you engage actively with the opportunities and challenges of life.

In addition, you get to grasp a sense of control and existence. You will become more aware of your own presence and acknowledge your significance. Expect to bring back your sense of control over your own actions and choices, too. With that, you will enjoy a more purposeful and balanced life at your age.

Ikigai During Your Retirement Age

Your life during your retirement age should be filled with happy memories, instead of regrets and frustrations, and you can make that possible by still living with a sense of purpose even at that age. One thing you should remember about being a human being is that we will naturally age. Aging will always form a natural part of living.

However, there are things that can greatly affect and influence the way you age, including your lifestyle, sense of purpose, and mindset. It is in this area where you can expect the Japanese concept to come into play. The fact that this concept literally means your reason from being means that it represents your guiding principle once you reach your later years.

With that, you will enjoy a graceful aging process plus you get to maintain your physical, emotional, and mental well-being.

Healthy Aging Through Ikigai

One great thing about Ikigai is that it does not only work in your quest for the things you love and the things you are good at. Your Ikigai will also provide you with a purposeful life capable of bringing the kind of fulfillment and joy you are hoping for. Such a sense of purpose is extremely beneficial as soon as you age.

By strengthening your sense of purpose through Ikigai, you can enjoy several health benefits, like better mental health, higher longevity, and a lower chance of developing diseases. The fact that you will be required to align your long-term and short-term goals, as well as your everyday activities with your Ikigai, can also help you cultivate a kind of lifestyle, which leads to healthy aging.

Finding your Ikigai is also a major contributor to better physical, mental, and emotional health as you age. In terms of your mental health, it can benefit you as it ensures that your mind stays engaged and active. The reason is that you will be doing activities that are in line with your Ikigai, thereby giving you the mental stimulation you need and preventing cognitive decline. Some examples of these everyday activities are doing your hobby, learning a skill, or contributing to society.

In terms of your emotional health, you can expect your Ikigai to provide you with a sense of satisfaction and fulfillment. You get to retain a positive perspective on life since you can handle the emotional issues that usually result from aging.

Your Ikigai can also improve your physical health and wellness since you will be doing activities that boost your physical health and make you active. It could be through yoga, dancing, walking, gardening, or any other joyful physical activity. All these activities can lead to you aging gracefully and enjoying better well-being.

How to Use Ikigai to Deal with Age-related Concerns and Challenges?

Once you start to age, it is inevitable for you to encounter several challenges. The good news is that your knowledge of Ikigai can give you the kind of framework necessary to cope with such challenges. One thing you can do is to remain active. Look for physical activities that resonate with your identified Ikigai. You should then make them part of your everyday routine.

It also helps to stay connected even as you reach your age. Maintain your social connections then do activities that let you contribute to the society and community. Keep yourself engaged, too, as this is also the key to maintaining an active mind. In this case, you can pursue your hobbies, take on new and different challenges, and learn new skills linked to your Ikigai. It is also a great idea to try maintaining your positive perspective and outlook and find happiness in your daily activities.

Planning a Great Retirement Through Ikigai

Retirement plays a crucial milestone in your life. It does not only mark the end of your long work journey but also the start of another phase of your life. The problem is that retirement planning seems to be so daunting and sometimes, even frustrating. In that case, you can seek the help of Ikigai to make the process easier.

If you use it in the context of your retirement, there is a high probability that it will shape your retirement plans while supplying you with direction and a sense of purpose. Keep in mind that retirement does not just mean that you are at the end of your professional career.

As a matter of fact, it is the start of a new chapter that gives you the freedom to pursue your interests, hobbies, and passions. With the help of Ikigai, you will learn about such interests and passions, providing you the clarity of vision in terms of how you want your retirement to appear.

Ikigai can play a huge role as you shape your retirement plans as it will serve as your guide as you make significant decisions. Let's say, for example, that you found out that your Ikigai is all about helping others. In that case, you may consider getting a part-time job or volunteering in a non-profit or charitable institution as you retire. You can also pursue a particular interest and spend more time on it just in case your identified Ikigai revolves around a certain interest or hobby.

Now, the question is how can you align your Ikigai with your retirement plans? Well, the first thing you ought to do is to do a self-reflection. Reflect not only on your life in general but also on your specific values, skills, talents, and passions. By doing that, you get to identify your Ikigai once again after hitting your retirement age.

After identifying your Ikigai, it helps to develop clear retirement goals that you can achieve at that age and ensure that it is in line with your Ikigai. You can then make a detailed plan providing detailed information on how you intend to achieve your retirement goals. During this stage, you will have several practical considerations, including time management and financial planning.

Your flexibility matters a lot as you reach your retirement age and practice Ikigai along the process, too. You should be flexible enough that you are willing to make adjustments to your plans whenever necessary. Also, note that even during your retirement age, your Ikigai can still evolve. In this case, you should improve your flexibility so you can accommodate the necessary changes and adjustments.

BONUS CHAPTER
Common Japanese Terms

Since Ikigai is a famous concept in Japan, this book provides a few Japanese terms with their meanings. That way, you can familiarize yourself with the Japanese language a bit.

Japanese Term	English Translation	Spelling in Japanese
konnichiwa	hello	こんにちは
hai	yes	はい
iie	no	いいえ
sumimasen	excuse me	すみません
watashi	i	私
kare	he	彼
kanojo	she	彼女
anata	you	あなた
ja ne	goodbye	じゃね
gomen nasai	i'm sorry	ごめんなさい
arigatou	thank you	ありがとう
sore	that	それ
kore	this	これ
karera	they	彼ら
mise	shop	店
kazoku	family	家族
ie or uchi	home	家
gakkou	school	学校
eiga	movie	映画
kuruma	car	車
toire	bathroom	トイレ

shusshin	hometown	出身
machi	town	町
ongaku	music	音楽
shigoto	job, work	仕事
iku	go	行く
ooi	many	多い
miru	look at, see	見る
deru	leave, go out	出る
tokoro	place	所
omou	think	思う
kau	buy	買う
jikan	hour, time	時間
shiru	know	知る
ima	now	今
atarashii	new	新しい
ato	after	あと
iu	tell, say	言う
kiku	ask, hear	聞く
kodomo	child	子供
sou	that way, so	そう
douzo	please	どうぞ
gakusei	student	学生
nagai	long	長い
kao	face	顔
owaru	end, finish	終わる
ageru	offer, give	あげる
hajimeru	start something	始める
haru	spring	春
sumu	reside, live	住む
sensei	teacher	先生

tatsu	rise, stand	立つ
kaeru	go back home	帰る
chikai	close, near	近い
suu	number	数
wakaru	understand	分かる
hiroi	big, wide	広い
hashiru	run	走る
kaku	write	書く
karada	physique, body	体
tobu	fly	飛ぶ
suki	liked, favorite	好き
yomu	read	読む
nomu	drink	飲む
shitsumon	question	質問
tomodachi	companion, friend	友達
hayai	early	早い
utsukushii	beautiful	美しい
miseru	show	見せる
tanoshimu	enjoy	楽しむ
iro	color	色
benkyou	study	勉強
dekiru	be good at, can do	できる
hikouki	airplane	飛行機
omoi	heavy	重い
mitsukeru	find	見つける
sake	rice wine, alcohol	酒
oboeru	learn, memorize	覚える
warau	smile, laugh	笑う
semai	narrow, small	狭い
shuu	week	週

densha	train	電車
kami	paper	紙
issho ni	together	一緒に
hayai	fast	速い
asobu	play	遊ぶ
yowai	weak	弱い
suwaru	sit down	座る
kesu	turn off	消す
genki	healthy	元気
hiku	pull, draw	引く
okuru	send	送る
kimochi	sensation, feeling	気持ち
noru	take, ride	乗る
iru	stay, be present	いる
matsu	wait	待つ
namae	name	名前
hanasu	talk, speak	話す
amai	sweet	甘い
tenki	weather	天気

Conclusion

At this stage of modern life where mounting stress and relentless speed are often the norm, you need to have a driving and motivational force that will keep you going forward. It should be something that will give your life meaning and inspire you to do better each day. In this case, you can take advantage of Ikigai, a Japanese concept rooted in their culture.

With the help of Ikigai, you will no longer yearn for your purpose and meaning since you will get to uncover it no matter what age or life stage you are in right now. You don't have to see yourself adrift in the present fast-paced world we are in right now. Your Ikigai will be the key to finally satisfying your cravings for connection with anything significant.

Hopefully, the contents of this book have helped you understand Ikigai even better. The knowledge you acquired from this book will surely guide you in using Ikigai as your pathway for rediscovering the essence of your life, fostering the kind of satisfaction and fulfillment you want as you align your everyday actions with passions and values.

As a result, you will finally be able to use Ikigai as your guiding philosophy that helps you pursue your dream career and uncover the value of each existing vocation. This will further result in you enjoying a more gratifying and sustainable experience with Ikigai acting as the catalyst for harmonizing professional and personal spheres.

Made in the USA
Monee, IL
14 February 2025